NHibernate 2
Beginner's Guide

Rapidly retrieve data from your database into .NET objects

Aaron B. Cure

[PACKT] open source
PUBLISHING
community experience distilled

BIRMINGHAM - MUMBAI

NHibernate 2
Beginner's Guide

Copyright © 2010 Packt Publishing

First published: May 2010

Production Reference: 1050510

Published by Packt Publishing Ltd.
32 Lincoln Road
Olton
Birmingham, B27 6PA, UK.

ISBN 978-1-847198-90-7

www.packtpub.com

Cover Image by Louise Barr (lou@frogboxdesign.co.uk)

Credits

Author

Aaron B. Cure

Reviewers

Jason Dentler

Fabio Maulo

Acquisition Editor

Usha Iyer

Development Editor

Chaitanya Apte

Technical Editor

Ajay B. Chamkeri

Copy Editor

Leonard D'Silva

Indexer

Monica Ajmera Mehta

Editorial Team Leader

Aanchal Kumar

Project Team Leader

Priya Mukerji

Project Coordinator

Ashwin Shetty

Proofreader

Lynda Sliwoski

Production Coordinator

Shantanu Zagade

Cover Work

Shantanu Zagade

About the Author

Aaron Cure is an avid developer, instructor, and innovator. During his 10 years in the military as a linguist and a satellite communications repair technician, he learned that his real love was computer programming.

After various throes with PHP, Classic ASP, VB, and a brief encounter with Java/JSP, he found a real passion for the .NET framework. After searching for a "better way" to carry out database storage and retrieval, Aaron stumbled across the NHibernate framework.

Unsatisfied with the options for interacting with this great framework, he founded the NHibernate Generation project (nhib-gen) on SourceForge to reduce the "barrier to entry" for most developers.

Aaron and his family run a small consulting and web hosting company doing web design and custom software development for various organizations across the country. One of their more interesting projects has been software to control laser cutting machines.

In his spare time, he also enjoys developing projects with his daughters, using everything from Lego NXT (using C# and Bluetooth communications) to the Microchip PIC platform (using JAL and USB). He also collects and restores classic farm tractors, engines, and farm equipment as well as semi trucks and trailers. He and his family display them at tractor shows, parades, schools, and various other community events.

This book is dedicated to my beautiful and talented wife, Sherry, and my two wonderful daughters, Kaitlyn and MacKenzie. Without their love and support, this book would have never been written.

I would also like to thank my parents, Karen and Chuck, as I wouldn't be here without them.

Special thanks to my editors at Packt Publishing, who had more patience with me than I think I would have had and stuck with me throughout.

About the Reviewers

Jason Dentler started tinkering with computers as a kid in the late 80s. As a college freshman, he got a job as an intern for a small call center company. Eight years later, he found himself coding for the entire call center division of a Fortune 500 company at their Global Technology Center in Las Vegas, Nevada. From there, he moved back to Texas and now works in higher education. He is an active participant in the NHibernate community and blogs about NHibernate, .NET, and programming in general at http://jasondentler.com.

> I'd like to thank my NHibernate friends Fabio, Tuna, Jose, and Oren for their support and mentorship, and Scott Guthrie, who with a single tweet, literally made my blog an overnight success.

Fabio Maulo is the NHibernate development team leader.

Table of Contents

Preface

NHibernate is a popular, fast growing **Object-Relational Mapper (ORM)** with a helpful community of seasoned developers. It is used in thousands of commercial and open source projects.

Armed with a set of simple (and mostly free) tools and the knowledge you'll gain from this book, you can quickly and easily create an entire data-bound website, desktop application, windows or web service, or virtually any other .NET project you can conceive.

What this book covers

Chapter 1, *First Look*, discusses what an object-relational mapper is, what NHibernate is, and the features it provides us.

Chapter 2, *Database Layout and Design*, discusses how your database is constructed, how the data is related, and how to optimize it for the best performance using NHibernate.

Chapter 3, *A Touch of Class*, explains how creating classes to represent your data makes it easy for you to work with the data and allows you to branch from the design of the database, if need be.

Chapter 4, *Data Cartography*, deals with the actual interface to the database with NHibernate, either using XML mapping files, Fluent NHibernate, or no mapping at all. We also talk about lazy loading, using a fieldnames structure to help avoid typos, and generating the database from our mapping files or classes.

Chapter 5, *The Session Procession*, teaches you how to create NHibernate sessions, which use database sessions to retrieve and store data into the database.

Chapter 6, *I'm a Logger*, teaches you how to use the log4net logging framework for creating our own logs and tap into the information provided by NHibernate (including SQL statements) to monitor and troubleshoot our application.

Chapter 7, Configuration, explains how to configure our application so, we are ready to retrieve and store data into our database. Additional configuration options are discussed, as well as optional configuration properties for particular situations.

Chapter 8, Writing Queries, discusses using NHibernate to actually retrieve data, to include individual records and collections of records. We talk about filtering records and using the fieldnames structure we created earlier to speed up our development. We also talk about adding parameters to make paging and sorting work in data-bound controls.

Chapter 9, Binding Data, explains how to use the data methods we created earlier to build a web application that uses our data access layer, the ObjectDataSource, and other data controls to retrieve, display, and even insert/update database data.

Chapter 10, NET Security Providers, presents information about controlling access to and restricting the usage of data within a .NET web application. We discuss the use of custom membership and role providers with NHibernate to control access to information.

Chapter 11, It's a Generation Thing, discusses how to use code generation techniques such as CodeSmith, NHib-Gen, and MyGeneration to automatically generate our data access layer to get us up and running that much quicker.

Chapter 12, Odds and Ends, discusses some advanced topics such as the Burrow session management framework and the NHibernate SchemaExport tool.

What you need for this book

To successfully complete the examples in this book, you will need a copy of either Visual Studio 2008 or 2010. You can use any version as long as it includes the web application projects. This could be either a Visual Web Developer Express version or any full version such as Professional.

In addition to Visual Studio, you will also need a SQL database server. The examples are generated using SQL Server Express 2008 and SQL Server Management Studio (SSMS) Express.

You will also need to download the NHibernate binary files from `sourceforge.net`.

Who this book is for

This book is for new and seasoned developers of .NET web or desktop applications who want a better way to access database data. It is a basic introduction to NHibernate, with enough information to get a solid foundation in using NHibernate. Some advanced concepts are presented where appropriate to enhance functionality or in situations where they are commonly used.

Conventions

In this book, you will find several headings appearing frequently.

To give clear instructions on how to complete a procedure or task, we use:

Time for action – heading

1. Action 1

2. Action 2

3. Action 3

Instructions often need some extra explanation so that they make sense, so they are followed with:

What just happened?

This heading explains the working of tasks or instructions that you have just completed.

You will also find some other learning aids in the book, including:

Pop quiz – heading

These are short multiple choice questions intended to help you test your own understanding.

Have a go hero – heading

These set practical challenges and give you ideas for experimenting with what you have learned.

You will also find a number of styles of text that distinguish between different kinds of information. Here are some examples of these styles, and an explanation of their meaning.

Code words in text are shown as follows: "This will give us a new DLL project called `Ordering.Data` inside a folder named `Ordering`, which contains a solution named `Ordering`."

A block of code is set as follows:

```
using System;
using System.Collections.Generic;
using System.Text;

namespace Ordering.Data
{
    class OrderHeader
    {
    }
}
```

When we wish to draw your attention to a particular part of a code block, the relevant lines or items are set in bold:

```
public class OrderHeader
{
    public OrderHeader() { }
}
```

Any command-line input or output is written as follows:

```
07:18:08.295 [10] INFO NHibernate.Cfg.Configuration - Mapping resource:
Ordering.Data.Mapping.Address.hbm.xml
```

New terms and **important words** are shown in bold. Words that you see on the screen, in menus or dialog boxes for example, appear in the text like this: Right-click on the **Ordering. Console** application, and select **Add | New Item**.

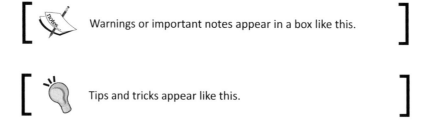

Warnings or important notes appear in a box like this.

Tips and tricks appear like this.

Reader feedback

Feedback from our readers is always welcome. Let us know what you think about this book—what you liked or may have disliked. Reader feedback is important for us to develop titles that you really get the most out of.

To send us general feedback, simply send an e-mail to feedback@packtpub.com, and mention the book title via the subject of your message.

If there is a book that you need and would like to see us publish, please send us a note in the **SUGGEST A TITLE** form on www.packtpub.com or e-mail suggest@packtpub.com.

If there is a topic that you have expertise in and you are interested in either writing or contributing to a book on, see our author guide on www.packtpub.com/authors.

Customer support

Now that you are the proud owner of a Packt book, we have a number of things to help you to get the most from your purchase.

Downloading the example code for the book

Visit https://www.packtpub.com//sites/default/files/downloads/8907_Code.zip to directly download the example code.

The downloadable files contain instructions on how to use them.

Errata

Although we have taken every care to ensure the accuracy of our content, mistakes do happen. If you find a mistake in one of our books—maybe a mistake in the text or the code—we would be grateful if you would report this to us. By doing so, you can save other readers from frustration and help us improve subsequent versions of this book. If you find any errata, please report them by visiting http://www.packtpub.com/support, selecting your book, clicking on the **let us know** link, and entering the details of your errata. Once your errata are verified, your submission will be accepted and the errata will be uploaded on our website, or added to any list of existing errata, under the Errata section of that title. Any existing errata can be viewed by selecting your title from http://www.packtpub.com/support.

Piracy

Piracy of copyright material on the Internet is an ongoing problem across all media. At Packt, we take the protection of our copyright and licenses very seriously. If you come across any illegal copies of our works, in any form, on the Internet, please provide us with the location address or website name immediately so that we can pursue a remedy.

Please contact us at `copyright@packtpub.com` with a link to the suspected pirated material.

We appreciate your help in protecting our authors, and our ability to bring you valuable content.

Questions

You can contact us at `questions@packtpub.com` if you are having a problem with any aspect of the book, and we will do our best to address it.

1
First Look

It seems like every single project we begin as developers, no matter how simple, requires some sort of storage. Sometimes this is a simple collection of values in an XML file or a key-value pair in a properties file.

However, more often, we need to have access to larger volumes of data, represented in multiple related database tables. In either case, we are generally forced to reinvent the wheel, to create new data retrieval and storage methods for each piece of data we want to access. Enter NHibernate.

In this chapter, we will discuss:

- ◆ What NHibernate is and why we should use it
- ◆ HBM mapping files
- ◆ Plain Old CLR Objects (POCOs)
- ◆ Data access classes
- ◆ A simple web page databound to a collection of NHibernate objects

What is NHibernate?

That's a great question, and I'm glad you asked! NHibernate is an open source persistence layer based on Object-Relational Mapping Techniques or simply a tool that creates a "virtual representation" of database objects within the code. According to the creators of NHibernate:

> NHibernate is a port of Hibernate Core for Java to the .NET Framework. It handles persisting plain .NET objects to and from an underlying relational database. Given an XML description of your entities and relationships, NHibernate automatically generates SQL for loading and storing the objects.

In simple terms, NHibernate does all the database work, and we reap all the benefits! Instead of writing reams of SQL statements or creating stored procedures that "live" in a different place than our code, we can have all of our data access logic contained within our application.

With a few simple "tricks" that we'll discuss in *Chapter 4, Data Cartography*, not only will our queries be effective, but they will also be validated by the compiler. Therefore, if our underlying table structure changes, the compiler will alert us that we need to change our queries!

Why would I use it?

Unless you love to write **CRUD (Create**, **Retrieve**, **Update**, **Delete)** methods over and over for each of the pieces of data you need to access (and I don't know a single developer who does), you are probably looking for a better method. If you're like me, then you know how to lay down an elegant database design (and if you don't, take a peek at *Chapter 2, Database Layout and Design*). Once the database is ready, you just want to use it!

Wouldn't it be nice to create a few tables, and in just a few minutes, have a working set of forms that you can use for all of your basic CRUD operations, as well as a full set of queries to access the most common types of data? We'll discuss some of the ways to automatically generate your NHibernate data files in *Chapter 11, It's a Generation Thing*.

Where do I get it?

The home of the NHibernate project is at `http://www.nhforge.org`, while the code is housed at SourceForge (`http://sourceforge.net/projects/nhibernate/`).

If you download the latest **GA (Generally Available**, also known as final or stable) bin release (binaries only, no source code) of the NHibernate project, you will have everything you need to get started. As of this writing, the current release is NHibernate-2.1.2.GA-bin, and all of the examples have been developed using this version. This version is available at `http://downloads.sourceforge.net/project/nhibernate/NHibernate/ 2.1.2GA/NHibernate-2.1.2.GA-bin.zip`.

Can I get help using NHibernate?

There is a great community site for NHibernate on the Web called the NHibernate Forge. It is located at `http://www.nhforge.org/`, and it provides a wealth of resources for the new and veteran NHibernate user.

Have a go hero – looking at some sample files

A basic NHibernate project is composed of three major parts. You will need a mapping file to tell NHibernate how the database is or should be (see the *Mapping our types* section in *Chapter 4*) constructed, some data access methods to tell NHibernate what data you want to retrieve or store into the database, and a POCO to allow you to interact with the data. While XML mapping files are commonly used in NHibernate projects, they are not the only way to map data to POCOs (more in *Chapter 4*).

Take a look at some sample files, but don't get too hung up on them. We'll go into more detail in the later chapters.

Database table

The first item we need to use NHibernate is a database table to map against. In the following screenshot, we define a table named **Login** with a Primary Key column named **Id**, two nullable fields to store the **FirstName** and **LastName**, and two non-nullable fields to store the **UserName** and **Password**.

Login		
Column Name	Data Type	Allow Nulls
🔑 Id	int	☐
FirstName	varchar(255)	☑
LastName	varchar(255)	☑
UserName	varchar(50)	☐
Password	varchar(50)	☐
		☐

The XML mapping file (hbm.xml)

The following code snippet shows the `Login.hbm.xml` mapping file for this simple table, with all the information required not only to map the data, but also to create the database from the metadata contained within the mapping file. If we do not want to be able to generate the database from the mapping file, then we can omit all of the `sql-type`, `unique`, and `index` properties.

Some immediate information you might pick up from the file are the name of the class that NHibernate will use to map database rows (`BasicWebApplication.Common.DataObjects.Login`), which is defined in the `<class>` tag. This says that the `BasicWebApplication.Common.DataObjects.Login` object is contained in the `BasicWebApplication` assembly. It further defines that the `Login` table is the database table we will be mapping to, using the `<table>` element.

There is an `<id>` tag that defines what the unique identifier (ID) is for the database record, as well as how that identifier is expected to be created. In our case, the `<generator class="hilo">` tag specifies that we will be using the hi/lo **Persistent Object ID (POID)** generator for IDs.

The four string fields `FirstName`, `LastName`, `UserName`, and `Password` are then mapped to the four database columns of the same names, using the `<property>` tag.

```xml
<?xml version="1.0" encoding="utf-8" ?>
<hibernate-mapping xmlns="urn:nhibernate-mapping-2.2"
  namespace="BasicWebApplication.Common.DataObjects"
  assembly="BasicWebApplication">
  <class name="Login" table="Login">
    <id name="Id" type="Int32" unsaved-value="null">
      <column name="Id" />
      <generator class="hilo" />
    </id>
    <property name="FirstName" type="String" />
    <property name="LastName" type="String" />
    <property name="UserName" type="String" />
    <property name="Password" type="String" />
  </class>
</hibernate-mapping>
```

Plain Old CLR Object (POCO)

The `Login.cs` class shown in the following code snippet is the POCO, the class that NHibernate will use to map database rows. Each row in the database returned will be instantiated (also known as "newed up") in a new instance of the `Login` class. The collection of rows will be returned as a generic `IList` of `Login` objects or an `IList<Login>`.

Notice how each property in the class `Login` maps directly to a property element in the `hbm.xml` file. We really have five public properties on this object, `Id`, `FirstName`, `LastName`, `UserName`, and `Password`. Each of these properties was defined earlier in the `hbm.xml` file and mapped to a database field.

When NHibernate retrieves records from the database, it will create a new instance (also known as "new up") of a `Login` object for each record it retrieves and use the public "setter" (set function) for each property to fill out the object.

```
public partial class Login
{
  public Login() { }

  public virtual int Id { get; set; }
  public virtual string FirstName { get; set; }
  public virtual string LastName { get; set; }
  public virtual string UserName { get; set; }
  public virtual string Password { get; set; }
}
```

Data access

The final class, `LoginDataControl.cs`, provides CRUD methods for data retrieval, storage, and removal. The session variable is an NHibernate session (you can find out more about session management in *Chapter 5, The Session Procession*).

This class defines a few simple CRUD methods that are used quite often when manipulating database records. The `GetById(int id)` function allows the user to pass in an integer and retrieve the record with that ID. The `GetAll()` method returns all of the records in a given table. `GetCountOfAll()` returns a count of the records in the table, while allowing controls that handle pagination and record navigation to function.

```
public class LoginDataControl
{
  public LoginDataControl() { }
  ISession session;
```

```
public Login GetById(int id)
{
  Login retVal = session.Get<Login>(id);
  return retVal;
}

public IList<Login> GetAll()
{
  ICriteria criteria = session.CreateCriteria<Login>();
  IList<Login> retVal = criteria.List<Login>();
  return retVal;
}

public int GetCountOfAll()
{
  return GetAll().Count;
}
}
```

Look how easy it is to use!

The sample `Login.aspx` ASP.NET file shows one of the best reasons why we use NHibernate. By using an ObjectDataSource, we can map the NHibernate objects directly to the data-bound controls that will display or interact with them. All we have to do is create an ObjectDataSource to retrieve the data from our data access class (`LoginDataControl.cs`), create a set of form fields to display the data (like the `<asp:GridView>` "LoginGrid" below), and let ASP.NET handle all of the tedious work for us. By the way, this page will work exactly as shown—there is no page logic in the code behind or anywhere else.

All we have in this code is a GridView to present the information and an ObjectDataSource to interact with our DataAccess classes and provide data for the GridView. The GridView has BoundField definitions for all of the fields in our database table as well as Sorting and Paging functions. The ObjectDataSource has methods mapped for `Select`, `Select Count`, `Insert`, and `Update`. When the GridView needs to perform one of these functions, it relies on the ObjectDataSource to handle these operations. Working in tandem, these two controls (as well as nearly any other data bound control) can provide a very quick and simple interface for your data!

```
<%@ Page Language="C#" AutoEventWireup="true"
  CodeBehind="Default.aspx.cs"
  Inherits="BasicWebApplication.Web._Default" %>

<!DOCTYPE html PUBLIC "-//W3C//DTD XHTML 1.0 Transitional//EN"
  "http://www.w3.org/TR/xhtml1/DTD/xhtml1-transitional.dtd">
```

```html
<html xmlns="http://www.w3.org/1999/xhtml">
  <head runat="server">
    <title>Untitled Page</title>
  </head>
  <body>
    <form id="form1" runat="server">
      <asp:GridView ID="LoginGrid" AutoGenerateColumns="false"
        DataSourceID="LoginSource" runat="server">
        <Columns>
          <asp:HyperLinkField HeaderText="ID" DataTextField="Id"
            SortExpression="Id" DataNavigateUrlFields="Id"
            DataNavigateUrlFormatString=
            "~/SampleForms/Login.aspx?LoginId={0}"
            Target="_parent" />
          <asp:BoundField HeaderText="FirstName"
            DataField="FirstName" />
          <asp:BoundField HeaderText="LastName"
            DataField="LastName" />
          <asp:BoundField HeaderText="UserName"
            DataField="UserName" />
          <asp:BoundField HeaderText="Password"
            DataField="Password" />
        </Columns>
      </asp:GridView>
    <asp:ObjectDataSource ID="LoginSource"
      TypeName="BasicWebApplication.DataAccess.LoginDataControl"
      DataObjectTypeName=
      "BasicWebApplication.Common.DataObjects.Login"
      SelectMethod="GetAll" SelectCountMethod="GetCountOfAll"
      runat="server"></asp:ObjectDataSource>
    </form>
  </body>
</html>
```

Summary

In this chapter, we talked a little bit about what NHibernate is, and why we should use it. We also touched on what **HBM mapping files** are and what they are used for, as well as the **Plain Old CLR Objects (POCOs)** that NHibernate actually maps data into. Neither of these would be very helpful to us without some **Data Access Object (DAO)** classes to tell NHibernate to retrieve or save the data we are working with. Finally we looked at a simple web page that was databound to a collection of NHibernate objects, all without any codebehind or other additional code.

It may seem like creating all these files is a lot of work, and it might be simpler to just go back to handcoding the SQL! I would tend to agree with you, if I didn't know the *shortcut* to creating all of these files—code generation, or even better, using Fluent NHibernate! If you can't wait, then sneak a peek at *Chapter 4, Data Cartography*, for more about Fluent NHibernate.

Now that we have skimmed the surface on how NHibernate works and how to make it work for us, let's talk about database layout and design, which is the subject of our next chapter.

2
Database Layout and Design

Like the foundation of a building, the structure of your database forms the base for your entire application. If you take a little care and build it well, then your overall experience with any data access technology will be greatly improved.

In this chapter, we'll discuss:

- ◆ Table layouts
- ◆ NHibernate assigned IDs
- ◆ Relationships
- ◆ Normal form

One of the most important things you can do in your project is to lay out your data in a logical and efficient model. In this chapter, we'll discuss the fundamentals of a good database design and how to model your data effectively.

Before you get started

The examples we are going to walk through in this and the following sections will work for Microsoft SQL Server Express. While you can use NHibernate against nearly any database on the planet (including MySQL, my personal favorite), SQL Server Express is available as a free download from Microsoft. If you happen to be working on a platform that cannot run SQL Server Express, I will provide some tips on making them work on other platforms.

Laying the foundation—table layouts

One of the most important things you can do from the beginning is to lay out your tables and entire data structure logically. Spending a few extra minutes in the beginning when designing a logical database can save you hours or even days worth of work later on. You would be surprised at the amount of time it takes to "work around" a bad database design, or worse, having to go back and "re-plumb" your data objects to make them work correctly.

The two rules I like to follow when creating a database are:

- Lay out objects in the database so that they are organized logically, either by the data they store or the business logic they represent
- Don't store duplicate data

For example, if we were trying to model an ordering system, we would need to store information about the order, the related customer, the products they ordered, their billing and shipping address, and so on. It would be simple enough to create a single table to store all of this data, but that would violate rule number two, as we would potentially have the same address, phone number product information, and so on stored over and over.
So how do we handle this?

Time for action – creating an ordering system database

So we want to build a simple ordering system. We are going to need to store the orders, the order items, the products they represent, the contact that placed the order, and the billing and shipping addresses. Let's get started!

1. If you haven't already, install the Microsoft SQL Server Express with Tools, or install Microsoft SQL Server Express and Microsoft SQL Server Management Studio Express (SSMS). If you don't have the .NET Framework 3.5 installed already, then you will need to install that before you will be able to install SSMS, as well as Windows PowerShell. We will use SSMS to design our database.

2. Open SSMS (**Start | All Programs | Microsoft SQL Server (version) | SQL Server Management Studio Express**).

3. When you open SSMS, you will be prompted for login credentials for the database. Generally, you can enter either the **hostname\SQLEXPRESS** or **(local)\SQLEXPRESS**.

 If you changed the name of the SQL Server instance when you installed SQL Server Express, you will need to use that instance name instead of SQLEXPRESS.

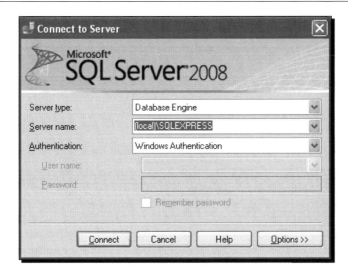

4. Leave authentication set at **Windows Authentication** and click on **Connect**.

5. You will be presented with a screen similar to the following screenshot. This shows a basic summary of the SQL Server instance that you are connected to, such as the databases on the server, security information (logins, roles), and so on.

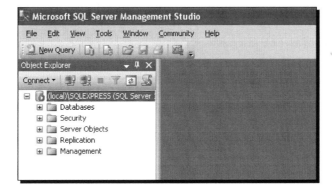

6. Now, we will create our "Ordering" database. Right-click on the **Databases** folder, and click on **New Database**.

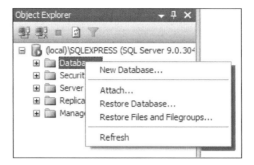

7. Enter the name **Ordering** for the **Database name**, and accept the default values, then click on **OK** to create the database.

 If you want to change the location where the database is physically stored, you can move the slider at the bottom of the form over to the right and adjust the "Path" settings.

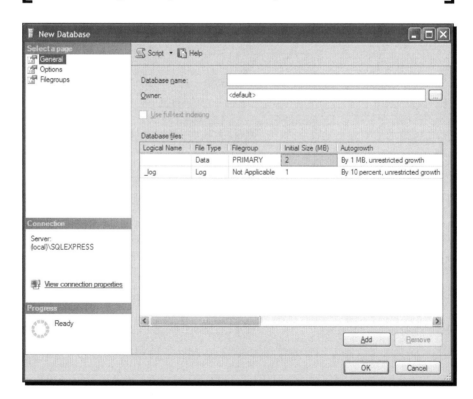

8. Now that we have a database created, we can explore it a little on the left-hand side in the **Object Explorer** by clicking the **+** next to **Databases** and the one next to our **Ordering** database.

9. You will see the collapsed folders for **Tables** and **Views**, as well as **Database Diagrams** and **Security**. These are the most common objects we will use within SSMS to create database objects and manage their security permissions.

What just happened?

We have just created our basic Ordering system database. We will continue to use this database throughout this chapter and throughout the entire book. A backup of this database is available for you to restore in the file `2.1 - Ordering.bak`.

Now that we have our database, we can move on to creating a structure to store our data!

Table layouts

Creating a table layout is a little like art, but don't worry if you're not a "Da Vinci"! If you follow some basic guidelines about table design, you will do just fine.

One of the most important things you can do when you design your tables is give them a good name. The name of the table should describe what types of records and data it is meant to hold. Remember, unless you change it, the name you give your object in the database is the name you will use to refer in the code. Do you really want to create an "S-9619" object every time you create an order, or does creating a "BillOfLading" object make more sense? I think just about every developer in the world would agree that more descriptive names, even if it means a little more typing, make the database structure more understandable and the eventual code more readable in the end.

Table names should be singular, like the objects they represent. Each row of the table in the database will represent a single object such as a "Contact" or a "BillOfLading" or an "order_item".

Each column in the database is called a field. Field names should follow a similar form as tables. A "CountryOfOrigin" or "country_of_origin" field makes more sense to someone viewing (and even to you at 3AM!) than a field named "3412". Make your field names descriptive so they remind you of what you intend to store in there.

The first field you define should be your Primary Key. The Primary Key of a table acts as the Identifier for that row. By defining the field as a Primary Key, we are saying that this value is used to uniquely identify *this* row and is NOT a natural key (that is, SSN or phone number).

A Primary Key should have a few basic attributes:

- Be defined as an integer, long, or GUID (not a VARCHAR!)
- Not allow nulls
- Be unique
- Be declared as the Primary Key
- Be assigned by an NHibernate POID (Persistent Object ID) generator

Take a look at the table shown in the following screenshot. This table defines a **Contact** object, with a Primary Key (notice the key icon) called **Id** defined as an integer, and the other fields, each defined as a varchar (string), and the **Email** field is required (it doesn't allow nulls).

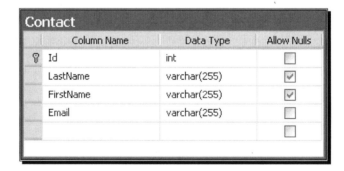

NHibernate assigned IDs

One of the criteria for a good Primary Key is that it is assigned by an NHibernate POID generator. Automatic assignment lets NHibernate manage the assignment of Primary Keys. NHibernate has the "smarts" baked right in to create those IDs for us and put them back into our object.

Whenever a record is inserted into the database, it is assigned a number, either the next number in the sequence (that is, hi/lo), or a randomly assigned GUID (Globally Unique Identifier), depending on which POID you are using. We will talk more about POID generators in *Chapter 4, Data Cartography*.

Relationships

One of the goals of our database design is to reduce the duplication of data and logically group different types of data into different tables. A logical separation would be for things like contacts. If we wanted to store all of our contacts, their phone numbers, addresses, and so on, then we could store it in a table, as shown in the following screenshot:

Contact		
Column Name	Data Type	Allow Nulls
Id	int	☐
LastName	varchar(255)	☑
FirstName	varchar(255)	☑
Email	varchar(255)	☐
Address1	varchar(255)	☐
Address2	varchar(255)	☑
City	varchar(255)	☐
State	varchar(2)	☐
Zip	varchar(12)	☐
Phone	varchar(20)	☑
		☐

At first glance, this looks like a pretty elegant solution that would work fine. What if I want to store a contact without an address? Can I do this? Currently the table doesn't allow NULL values in the address fields, so I would have to change that. How about storing more than one address like a work and a home address? What about multiple phone numbers? The list goes on. What we really need here is a way to logically store grouped data in its own table, and relate it to other pieces of data. This is called a relationship, and it is probably the single most powerful concept in database design ever. By allowing a relational database to store metadata, or data about the data, we can now say that table A stores data in common with table B, but there may be zero or more records for table B in table A. Makes sense? It will.

There are a few common types of relationships you need to know about, the **one-to-many** (**OTM**), its logical inverse cousin the **many-to-one** (**MTO**), the **one-to-one** (**OTO**), and the **many-to-many** (**MTM**). Just like their names imply, these relationships define how the data relates to the other data. OTO relationships are fairly uncommon and can usually be modeled directly within the base table.

Take a look at the following two tables. They represent a typical OTM relationship, represented by the key (denoting the Primary Key) and the infinity (∞) symbol (denoting the Foreign Key).

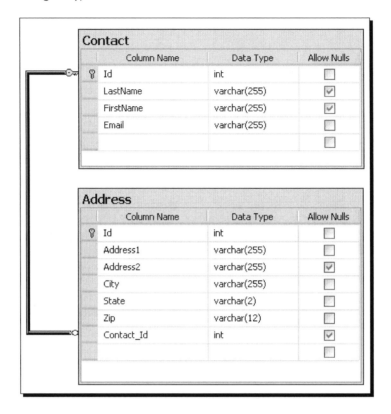

In an OTM relationship, the relationship information is stored on the "Many" side, that is, the field called **Contact_Id**. We will store the data from the **Id** column of the related contact from the Contact table. As you will see in the following table, we have some contacts already stored in our table with auto-numbered IDs.

Id	LastName	FirstName	Email
1	King	Riley B.	NULL
2	Bailey	William	NULL
3	Pincus	Barry Alan	NULL
4	Crosby	Harry Lillis	NULL
▶*	NULL	NULL	NULL	NULL

If you look at the data in the **Address** table, you will notice that we have addresses for two of our contacts, Mr. King and Mr. Bailey (see the **Contact_Id** field to match them up with the **Id** field in the **Contact** table).

Id	Address1	Address2	City	State	Zip	Contact_Id
1	P.O. Box 26867	NULL	Las Vegas	NV	89126	1
2	8295 South La Cienega Blvd	NULL	Inglewood	CA	90301	2
*	NULL NULL	NULL	NULL	NULL	NULL	NULL

If we wanted to see this data together, then we could execute a SQL query in the following manner:

```
select *
from Contact
join Address on Address.Contact_Id = Contact.Id
```

We have instructed the database to return all rows from the database where **Contact_Id** in the Address table equals the **Id** field in the Contact table. This should return four rows, one for each contact in the database. The following screenshot shows the output from this command:

Id	LastName	FirstName	Email	Id	Address1	Address2	City	State	Zip	Contact_Id
1	King	Riley B.	NULL	1	P.O. Box 26867	NULL	Las Vegas	NV	89126	1
2	Bailey	William	NULL	2	8295 South La Cienega Blvd	NULL	Inglewood	CA	90301	2

What happened to our other two rows? Why didn't they show up? SQL did exactly what we told it to do, to join the two tables and show all the rows that are in common between the two tables. If we don't specify a specific type of join, then SQL will automatically do an Inner join, or in other words, it will just show rows that are common in both tables. What we didn't do is tell it to show us all of the Contact rows regardless of whether or not we have addresses for them. To show this data, we need to add the Left operator to return all of the rows from the table on the Left of the query. We could also use Right if we wanted all the Addresses and didn't care if there were Contacts associated with them. The result of this modified query is as follows:

```
select *
from Contact
left join Address on Address.Contact_Id = Contact.Id
```

Adding the `left` keyword (the Contact table we are joining to) returns the following output:

	Id	LastName	FirstName	Email	Id	Address1	Address2	City	State	Zip	Contact_Id
1	1	King	Riley B.	NULL	1	P.O. Box 26867	NULL	Las Vegas	NV	89126	1
2	2	Bailey	William	NULL	2	8295 South La Cienega Blvd	NULL	Inglewood	CA	90301	2
3	3	Pincus	Barry Alan	NULL	NULL	NULL	NULL	NULL	NULL	NULL	NULL
4	4	Crosby	Harry Lillis	NULL	NULL	NULL	NULL	NULL	NULL	NULL	NULL

The second most common type of relationship is the MTM table. This type of relationship models data where multiple records on the left are related to multiple records on the right. An example might be phone numbers. You and I might have the same work number because we work at the same company or my wife and I might have the same home phone number. Using an MTM relationship, we can model this data using an extra table to store the relationship information. The relationship would look something like the following screenshot:

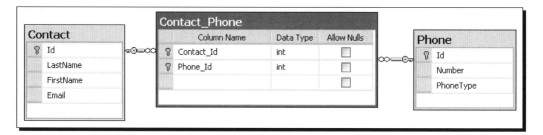

The **Contact_Phone** table links the **Contact** and **Phone** tables together. An MTM table implements two OTM relationships to complete the model. Notice that the **Contact_Phone** table has two keys, both **Contact_Id** and **Phone_Id**. This is called a Composite Primary Key and is used to mean that it takes both fields to make a record unique.

To create a Composite Primary Key, we simply select both the fields that we want to include in our Composite Primary Key before we designate it as a Primary Key.

To query this data, we would use a SQL statement as follows:

```
select *
from Contact
join Contact_Phone on Contact_Phone.Contact_Id = Contact.Id
join Phone on Contact_Phone.Phone_Id = Phone.Id
```

Armed with these two types of relationships, we can model 99.9 percent of all the data we need to store in nearly any project we come across.

Pop quiz – relationships

1. Which of the following is NOT a relational database relationship type?

    a. one-to-many (OTM)

    b. many-to-many (MTM)

    c. many-to-one (MTO)

    d. one to Several (OTS)

2. Which relationship type requires a secondary table to store the relationship data?

    a. one-to-many (OTM)

    b. many-to-many (MTM)

3. Which of the following is a VALID SQL join modifier?

    a. Left

    b. Right

    c. Inner

    d. All of the above

Normal Form

You may have heard the term **Third Normal Form** (**3NF**) when talking about databases and wondered what it meant. Quite simply, **Normalization** is a way to construct databases to standardize their appearance and to reduce duplication of data. Of the six normal forms (1st-5th and Boyce-Codd Normal Form or BCNF, another name for 3NF), 3NF is the most widely discussed, but **First Normal Form** (**1NF**) is the one we are most concerned with.

To be 1NF compliant, we need to eliminate duplicative columns from the same table, and create separate tables for each group of related data and identify each row with a unique column or set of columns (the Primary Key). In other words, we don't want to store duplicate data, we want to store it once and relate to it.

Essentially a 3NF database will store data in multiple tables to normalize the data and reduce duplication as we talked about earlier, and additionally:

◆ Functional dependencies on non-key fields are eliminated by putting them in a separate table. At this level, all non-key fields are dependent on the Primary Key.

◆ A row is in 3NF if and only if it is in Second Normal Form (2NF) and if attributes that do not contribute to a description of the Primary Key are moved into a separate table.

Have a go hero – looking back

Take a look at the second image (with the two tables Contact and Address) under the *Relationships* section again. Is this database in a 3NF design? Does it conform to all the rules of 3NF? If not, then how could we change the structure to accommodate 3NF? Does it make sense to make these changes or do we just want to live with the duplicated data?

Putting it all together

Now that we have all the concepts of database tables and relationships sorted out, let's add some tables to our Ordering system.

Time for action – adding some tables to our Ordering system database

Let's get back to our Ordering system. If you remember, we will need a table to store the orders and one for the order items. Let's build those now!

1. Open up SSMS again and log in to your local database server—(local)\SQLExpress.

2. Click on the **+** next to the **Ordering** database so we can see the objects in our database.

3. Right-click on the **Tables** folder, and click on **New Table** to bring up the new table dialog tab. This is where we will define our first table.

4. The new table editor tab will look similar to the table in the following screenshot. In the **Column Name** box, enter **Id**, either type or select **int** in the **Data Type** field, and uncheck the **Allow Nulls** checkbox.

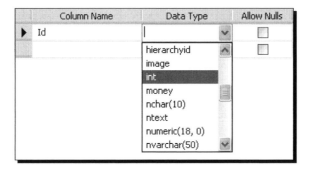

5. Next we need to set our "Primary Key" on this field. Right-click on the black arrow to the left of the **Id** column, and select **Set Primary Key** from the drop-down menu.

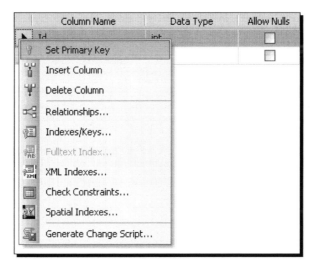

 Going forward, we will complete steps 3 through 5 to create a new table. We can call these steps our "Create a new table" process. In the future, whenever you need to create a table, these are the steps you will need to complete.

6. As we are creating a table to hold our orders, we will need to add some fields to store that data. Let's first create a field to hold an order number. Technically, we could just use the unique number from the Id field, but customers usually like to see something like "MUSA-2133-0623" as an order number, so we will create a varchar (string) field 255 characters in length. In the **Column Name** field, type **Number**, the **Data Type** field will be **varchar** and in place of the (50) it defaults to, replace the 50 with 255 so we can store a slightly longer order number.

	Column Name	Data Type	Allow Nulls
🔑	Id	int	☐
▶	Number	varchar(255)	☐
			☐

Fields constructed with data types such as varchar and varbinary can be defined as slightly larger than you plan to use them because they will only take up as much room for storage as the data that is in them. The "var" stands for variable. If you define the field as char(25) and store the words "hello world" in it, then the char field will take up 25 characters of disk space. If you use a varchar(25) and store the words "hello world" in them, it will take up only 11 characters of disk space.

7. Let's go ahead and add an **OrderDate** field as a **datetime**, and an **ItemQty** field as **int**. We will use these fields to store information about when the order was placed and the total number of items on the order.

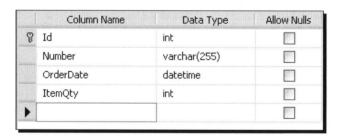

	Column Name	Data Type	Allow Nulls
🔑	Id	int	☐
	Number	varchar(255)	☐
	OrderDate	datetime	☐
	ItemQty	int	☐
▶			☐

8. We'll add a **Total** column for the Order as a decimal with 18 places before the decimal point and two after.

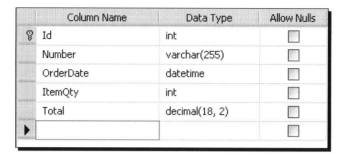

	Column Name	Data Type	Allow Nulls
🔑	Id	int	☐
	Number	varchar(255)	☐
	OrderDate	datetime	☐
	ItemQty	int	☐
	Total	decimal(18, 2)	☐
▶			☐

9. Finally, we need to save our table and give it a name. You can save the file by clicking on the Save (floppy disk) icon, pressing *Ctrl + S*, or selecting **File | Save Table_1**. Any of these options will bring up the following Save Table dialog box, which will prompt us to choose a name for our table:

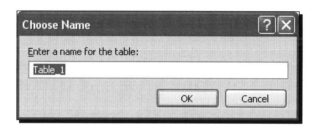

10. Enter the name **OrderHeader** (we can't use the name "Order" because Order is a reserved word in SQL), and click on **OK**.

 We will avoid using either SQL or .NET reserved words as our table or field names to save us trouble later when we try to use these tables in our .NET or SQL code.

11. If you click the refresh button (two arrows pointing in a circle) near the top of the "Object Explorer", and then use the **+** buttons to navigate to the **Tables** folder of the **Ordering** database, you should see our new "OrderHeader" table there. Open up that folder, and you should see a **Columns** folder. After opening that, you should be able to see all the columns we created, as shown in the following screenshot:

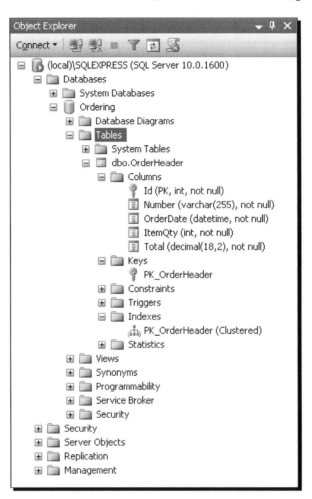

12. You will also notice that under the **Keys** folder, you can see our Primary Key definition for the Id column. SSMS also created a Clustered Index for our Primary Key.

If we wanted to, we could have scripted the creation of this table using SQL. Creating the table in SQL would look something like this:

```
CREATE TABLE [dbo].[OrderHeader](
        [Id] [int] NOT NULL,
        [Number] [varchar](255) NOT NULL,
        [OrderDate] [datetime] NOT NULL,
        [ItemQty] [int] NOT NULL,
    [Total] [decimal](18, 2) NOT NULL,
    CONSTRAINT [PK_OrderHeader] PRIMARY KEY CLUSTERED);
```

13. Now to create the OrderItem table. Perform our "Create new table" process to start our new OrderItem table. Add in the additional columns until your table looks similar to the table shown in the following screenshot:

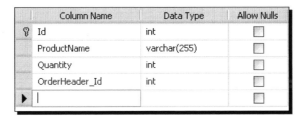

14. Next, we want to create the OTM relationship from OrderHeader to OrderItem. We need to link the 'Many' side (OrderItem.OrderHeader_Id) to the One side (OrderHeader.Id). To do this, we just right-click to the left of the **OrderHeader_Id** field and select **Relationships**, as shown in the following screenshot:

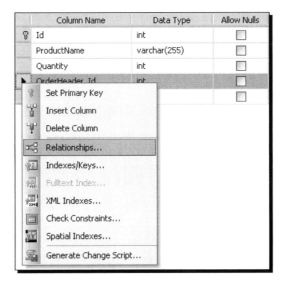

15. In the Relationships window, click on **Add**. This will create a new relationship called **FK_Table_1_Table_1**. This means that the Foreign Key relationship is from Table_1 to Table_1. Don't worry about the name right now, as it will change once we select our fields.

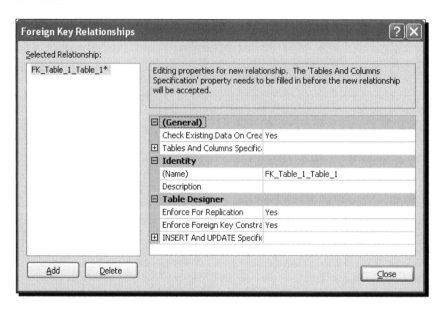

16. Click on the **Tables And Columns Specification** box and a set of ellipses (...) will appear. Click on the ellipses and the **Tables and Columns** window will appear. Open the **Id** drop-down under the **Foreign key table** column and select our Foreign key column, **OrderHeader_Id**. Click on one of the boxes under this column to "deselect" the drop-down.

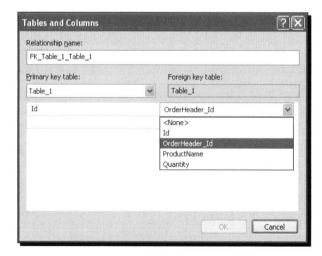

17. Under the **Primary key table** column, select the table **OrderHeader** from the drop-down that says **Table_1**, and select the **Id** field from the field selection below that. You should end up with a relationship that looks as shown in the following screenshot:

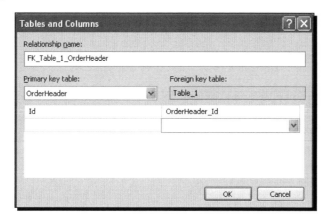

18. Finish the relationship creation by clicking on **OK** and then **Close** on the **Foreign Key Relationships** screen.

19. Save the table with the name **OrderItem**.

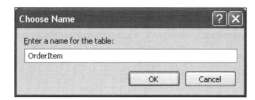

When you are prompted to save the changes to the two tables, click on **Yes**.

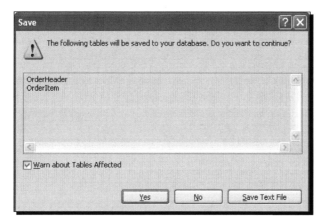

20. Refresh the **Object Explorer**, and you should be able to see both of our tables under the **Tables** folder of the **Ordering** database.

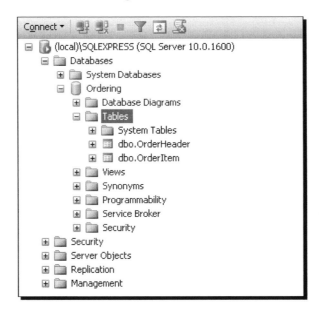

What just happened?

Now that we have created our OrderHeader and the related OrderItem tables, we are ready to start entering orders in our system! Our tables are fully functional, with data columns, Primary Keys, relationships, the works! The only thing left to do is get some customers to enter some orders, right?

Have a go hero – create some more tables

Now that you are a professional at creating tables and relationships, try adding the tables shown in the second image and the tables shown in the last image under the *Relationships* section to our Ordering database.

Create four fields on our OrderHeader to connect these tables: BillToContact_Id, ShipToContact_Id, BillToAddress_Id, and ShipToAddress_Id, and create relationships between the Contact and Address tables as appropriate.

Summary

So far, we talked about the right and wrong ways to create tables and fields!

Specifically, we covered:

- Creating our database table layouts and laying them out logically
- What Normal Form means and how we use it to design out database tables
- Using NHibernate assigned ID's to create Primary Key values for our database tables
- Defining various types of relationships to "connect" our related data

We also discussed Primary and Foreign keys and a little about the best ways to model data.

Now that we've learned about modeling our data into tables, we are ready to talk about creating this model inside .NET, which is the topic of the next chapter.

3

A Touch of Class

One of the greatest things that NHibernate brings to us is the ability to work directly with objects instead of having to deal with DataSets or DataReaders. Before we can use these objects, however, we of course need to define them.

In this chapter, we'll discuss:

- Constructors
- Public properties and private variables
- Converting SQL database types to CLR types
- Properties for Foreign Key fields

Start up our applications

We're going to be using the database that we created in *Chapter 2, Database Layout and Design*, so if you haven't already logged in, go ahead and log on to the database server and bring up our Ordering database. We will be using Visual Studio again, so you might as well start that up while you are at it.

Creating objects

We will be interacting with our classes the entire time we are programming, so spending a little extra time up front is an investment that will pay dividends almost immediately. As long as we remember a few simple concepts, we will be able to make very quick work of creating these classes. (For an even quicker way to create them, sneak a peek at *Chapter 11, It's a Generation Thing*, about Code Generation!)

One of the first things we will need for our new classes is a constructor. Constructors are used to "new up" an object. You have probably seen or written syntax similar to the following example:

```
OrderHeader header = new OrderHeader();
```

Or in VB.NET:

```
Dim header As OrderHeader = New OrderHeader()
```

In this example, we are creating a new OrderHeader object. This object represents the OrderHeader table we created in our database. To create this new object, we need a constructor (in this case the "default" constructor). Our default constructor is simply a method with no return object defined, with the same name as our class (in C#) or the keyword New (in VB.NET). The default constructor in our class will look something like this:

```
/// <summary>
/// Create an OrderHeader object Empty Constructor
/// </summary>
public OrderHeader() { }
```

In VB.NET:

```
''' <summary>
''' Create a OrderHeader object Empty Constructor
''' </summary>
Public Sub New()
End Sub
```

Time for action – creating our first class

In order for NHibernate to automatically fill data into our classes, we need to have some classes for it to fill! Let's start out by creating our OrderHeader class to map the OrderHeader data into.

1. In a new instance of Visual Studio, select **File** | **New** | **Project**, as shown in the following screenshot:

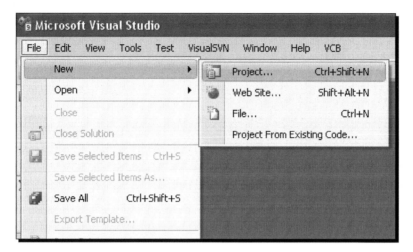

2. The **New Project** dialog will appear. If you are working in C#, select **Visual C#**, then **Windows**, and click on **Class Library**, as shown in the following screenshot:

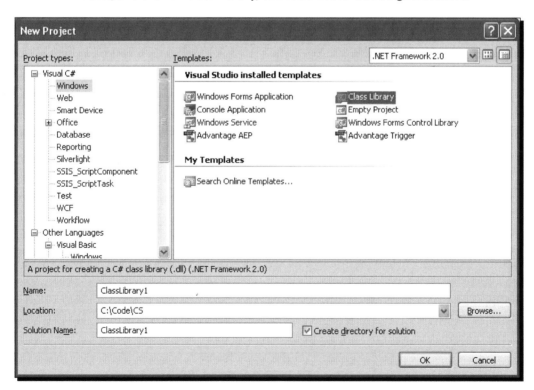

3. If you are a VB programmer, select **Visual Basic**, **Windows**, **Class Library**, as shown in the following screenshot:

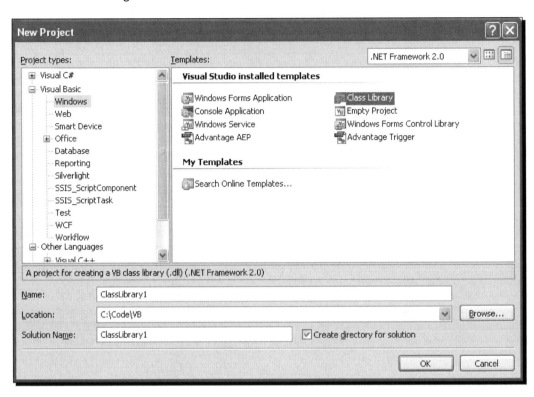

4. Enter **Ordering.Data** in the **Name:** textbox, and **Ordering** in the **Solution Name:** textbox. Make sure you leave the **Create directory for solution** checked.

5. This will give us a new DLL project called **Ordering.Data** inside a folder named **Ordering**, which contains a solution named Ordering. When you're done with it, the folder structure should look similar to the one shown in the following screenshot:

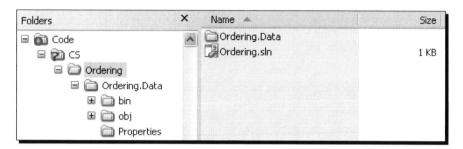

6. Right-click on the default new class that is automatically created (either Class1.cs or Class1.vb) and click **Delete**. We will be creating new classes and will not need this default class.

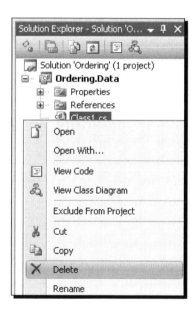

7. Now we want to create our `OrderHeader` class to represent the OrderHeader table in the database. Right-click on the **Ordering.Data** label underneath **Solution 'Ordering' (1 project)** and click **Add | Class**.

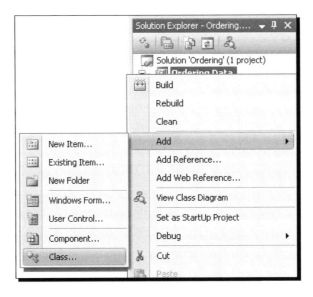

8. When the **Add New Item—Ordering.Data** dialog appears, **Class** will automatically be selected. In the **Name:** textbox, type **OrderHeader.cs**, and click on the **Add** button.

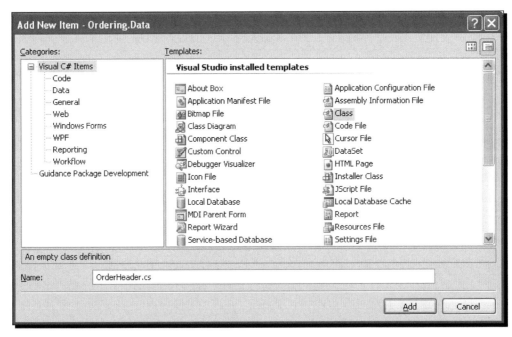

9. We will end up with a basic class to start off. The resulting document will look similar to the following code snippet:

```csharp
using System;
using System.Collections.Generic;
using System.Text;

namespace Ordering.Data
{
    class OrderHeader
    {
    }
}
```

 I personally like to add the `public` keyword to my classes when I want them to be public so there is no confusion, so I would change the preceding C# code to read:

```csharp
public class OrderHeader
```

Or in VB.NET, it will look as follows:

```vbnet
Public Class OrderHeader

End Class
```

10. Now we just need to add our default constructor logic. Between the curly braces (`{ }`) in C# or between the `Class` and `End Class` in VB.NET, we will add our logic.

```csharp
public class OrderHeader
{
    public OrderHeader() { }
}
```

And the corresponding VB.NET code:

```vbnet
Public Class OrderHeader
    Public Sub New()
    End Sub
End Class
```

11. Ensure that your code compiles by clicking on **Build | Rebuild Solution** or by pressing *Ctrl + Shift + B*.

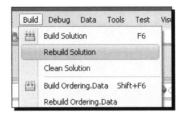

What just happened?

Congratulations! We just created our first class to allow NHibernate to map data into our application. We still have some work to do to get it to actually fill data, so let's keep going.

Have a go hero – ramping up

Now that we understand how to make some basic classes, we need to create them for the rest of our database. Try to create basic classes for the database tables we created in *Chapter 2*. The following screenshot shows the database diagram for our database:

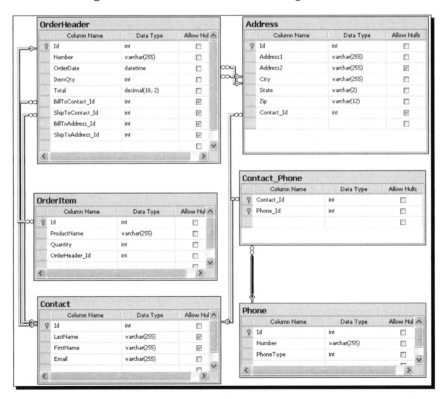

Public properties and private variables

NHibernate needs to have a place to "hold" the data that we are storing in the database. In order for NHibernate to do its job, we need to create some public properties to contain the data.

A property is simply a way to set and get data. We define a property by declaring a private variable to hold the actual data and some combination of a getter and/or a setter to manipulate the value in the private variable.

In C#, a property looks something as follows:

```
private int _id;
public int Id
{
  get { return _id; }
  set { _id = value; }
}
```

While in VB.NET, it will look as follows:

```
Private _id As Integer
Public Property Id() As Integer
  Get
    Return _id
  End Get
  Set(ByVal value As Integer)
    _id = value
  End Set
End Property
```

It is possible to create a ReadOnly property where a user has no access to the setter, that is, the only way to set the value is by manipulating the private variable from within the class itself. A ReadOnly property will look very similar to a property with a standard getter and setter. As you can see here, the C# code defines a ReadOnly property by simply omitting the setter.

```
private int _id;
public int Id
{
  get { return _id; }
}
```

In VB.NET, the property actually uses the `ReadOnly` keyword to denote that this property cannot be updated, as well as removing the "setter".

```
Private _id As Integer
Public ReadOnly Property Id() As Integer
  Get
    Return _id
  End Get
End Property
```

But what about those pesky Nullable properties? How do we handle those? While we can't put a `null` value for a value type (like an int), we can put one in a reference or generic type. Instead of using a value type of int in C#, we will use a nullable int (" `int?`") like this:

```
private int? test;
```

In VB.NET we actually use the `Nullable(of X)` notation, like this:

```
Private test As Nullable(Of Integer)
```

Now we're ready to get some work done!

Time for action – adding a few properties

Now that we have our simple `OrderHeader` class, we need to create some properties to actually hold our data. Let's get started.

Remember the OrderHeader table we created in *Chapter 2*, shown in the following screenshot? Let's add the **Id** and **Number** fields as properties in our class.

Column Name	Data Type	Allow Nulls
🔑 Id	int	☐
Number	varchar(255)	☐
OrderDate	datetime	☐
ItemQty	int	☐
Total	decimal(18, 2)	☐
BillToContact_Id	int	☑
ShipToContact_Id	int	☑
BillToAddress_Id	int	☑
ShipToAddress_Id	int	☑
		☐

1. Open the `OrderHeader` class that we created earlier in this chapter. There are numerous ways to create a property, but we'll start by just creating them manually. Under the default constructor we created earlier, let's create a private variable to hold the Id field. We will create these as private variables to hide the functionality from the end user, as we want them to use our properties.

 There is no hidden magic in using the underscore ("_") character as a prefix for the private variable. You can use "id", "m_Id", or virtually anything else you want.

2. In C#, we declare the variable as an `int`, which is a shortcut for `Int32`.

```
private int _id;
```

In VB.NET, we will declare the variable as an `Integer`.

```
Private _id As Integer
```

 If you are interested, play with the "Insert Snippet" dialog on the right-click menu. You can insert properties using this dialog fairly quickly.

3. Next, we need to create the property that will access our private variable. While properties can technically be created as private or protected, we will create standard public properties. We will mark these properties `virtual` or `Overridable` in VB.NET to allow lazy loading. We'll talk more about this later.

4. We will put our property under the private variable declaration from Step 1. Add the declaration of the public property as follows:

```
public virtual int Id
{
}
```

Here is the same code in VB.NET.

```
Public Overridable Property Id() As Integer
End Property
```

5. Next, we'll add our getter and setter. They simply use the `return` and `value` keywords, which are a sort of "magic" variables for properties.

Inside our previous property declaration, insert the getter and setter as follows:

```
get { return _id; }
set { _id = value; }
```

While the VB.NET code is a little more verbose, it does the same thing:

```
Get
   Return _id
End Get
Set(ByVal value As Integer)
   _id = value
End Set
```

That's it! Your finished `Id` property should look as follows:

```
private int _id;
public virtual int Id
{
   get { return _id; }
   set { _id = value; }
}
```

The VB.NET code is as follows:

```
Private _id As Integer
Public Overridable Property Id() As Integer
   Get
      Return _id
   End Get
   Set(ByVal value As Integer)
      _id = value
   End Set
End Property
```

6. Now let's add a property for the Number field in the database table. This field is declared as a `varchar(255)`, so we will create it as a collection of variable characters, or in .NET speak, we simply call it a `string`.

```
private string _number;
public string Number
{
   get { return _number; }
   set { _number = value; }
}
```

With a few more lines of code, the VB.NET code does the same thing:

```
Private _number As String
Public Property Number() As String
  Get
    Return _number
  End Get
  Set(ByVal value As String)
    _number = value
  End Set
End Property
```

7. The last thing we should do is add a constructor with our new properties so that we can "new up" an OrderHeader object and fill all the properties at the same time. Under our previous default constructor, let's add the following code:

```
public OrderHeader( string Number)
{
  this.Number = Number;
}
```

The same code in VB.NET is as follows:

```
Public Sub New(ByVal Number As String)
  Me.Number = Number
End Sub
```

8. The last thing we should do to our code, now that we are starting to get a few lines, is to wrap our major sections in Regions. **Regions** allow us to expand and collapse the code as well as provide quick headers to help us locate our code.

9. Between the class declaration and the default constructor, add a `Region` declaration as follows:

```
#region Constructors
```

Notice that in VB.NET, you have to put the text in quotes:

```
#Region "Constructors"
```

10. After our new constructor (just before the first property), we need to add an `End Region` directive to close it out:

```
#endregion
```

Once again, in VB.NET:

```
#End Region.
```

11. Add a region for the properties also, calling the region "Properties".

```
#region Properties
…
#endregion
```

Once again, in VB.NET:

```
#Region "Properties"
…
#End Region
```

12. That's it! We now have our first working class!

What just happened?

We're getting really close to mapping database data into our class with NHibernate now! We have constructors, properties, and even some regions that we can collapse and expand at will to make the code easier to read!

Converting SQL database types to .NET types

One of the things you will start to know as you play with it a little more is what types of data map into .NET types. In our examples before, an `int` in SQL Server became an `int` or `Integer`, while a `varchar` became a `String`. Some of the most common database types are listed in the following table, along with their associated .NET types.

Database type	.NET type
DbType.AnsiStringFixedLength - (char)	System.Char
DbType.Boolean (bool, bit)	System.Boolean
DbType.Byte	System.Byte
DbType.StringFixedLength - 1 char	System.Char
DbType.DateTime	System.DateTime
DbType.Decimal	System.Decimal
DbType.Double	System.Double
DbType.Guid	System.Guid
DbType.Int16 (short)	System.Int16
DbType.Int32 (int)	System.Int32
DbType.Int64 (long)	System.Int64
DbType.Single	System.Single
DbType.DateTime	System.DateTime
DbType.AnsiStringFixedLength - ('T' or 'F')	System.Boolean
DbType.AnsiStringFixedLength - ('Y' or 'N')	System.Boolean

These types will help you when you try to map the rest of the database fields to properties in our classes.

Properties for Foreign Keys

Okay, so we know how to map all of the basic fields now, but what about those pesky Foreign Key fields, such as BillToContact_Id? How do we map those guys? They're mapped as int in the database, so we can just map them as int or Integer, right?

Technically, we could map them as int in our code, but that would make our work much more difficult when we go to use the actual object, and the reason we are using NHibernate is to make our job EASIER!

What we really need to do is map these fields as objects. As each of these fields links to another table (BillToContact_Id stores the ID from Contact) we can map these fields as objects and actually view these related objects.

For example, the OrderItem table has a parent-child relationship to the OrderHeader table using the field OrderHeader_Id, which links this table to the OrderHeader table. If I was looking at an order (OrderHeader), I would want to see all the items on that order (OrderItem). If I want to look at all the order items and see if any have a quantity of more than five, for example, I could do something like this:

```
OrderHeader order = OrderHeaderDataControl.GetById(1);
foreach (OrderItem item in order.OrderItems)
{
    ...
}
```

As you can see, once I have the order, I can look at all the OrderItems simply by accessing the OrderItems property of the OrderHeader object. So, how do we define these you ask? Just like any other property, we are going to create a private variable and a public property. The type we assign to the property will be another class, the one to represent the other items. Because the Foreign Key could be one-to-many (OTM), many-to-many (MTM), or anything else, we will use a Generic List of objects to hold our collections.

Specifically, we will use the generic interface IList to group our objects because we can then cast it into any other collection that implements IList like an ArrayList to get sorting and filtering.

C# uses the `<>` identifier to denote Generic collections.

```csharp
private IList<OrderItem> _orderItems;
public IList<OrderItem> OrderItems
{
  get { return _orderItems; }
  set { _orderItems = value; }
}
```

In VB.NET, we need to use the `Of` keyword to create the generic IList of the type OrderItem.

```vbnet
Private _orderItems As IList(Of OrderItem)
Public Property OrderItems() As IList(Of OrderItem)
  Get
    Return _orderItems
  End Get
  Set(ByVal value As IList(Of OrderItem))
    _orderItems = value
  End Set
End Property
```

Now all that's left is to actually create the OrderItem class, and on that class, we will put an `OrderHeader` property so that we can navigate in code from the OrderItem back to its parent through this relationship. Instead of using a Generic List, we will just use an object as this will only hold a single OrderHeader instance.

```csharp
public class OrderItem
{
  public OrderItem() { }

  private OrderHeader _orderHeader;
  public OrderHeader OrderHeader
  {
    get { return _orderHeader; }
    set { _orderHeader = value; }
  }
}
```

In VB.NET, the code is as follows:

```vbnet
Public Class OrderItem
  Public Sub New()
  End Sub

  Private _OrderHeader As OrderHeader
  Public Property OrderHeader() As OrderHeader
```

```
     Get
        Return _OrderHeader
     End Get
     Set(ByVal value As OrderHeader)
        _OrderHeader = value
     End Set
  End Property
End Class
```

Now we're ready to map the rest of our classes!!

Have a go hero – adding more properties (and classes!)

Now that we have all of the skills we need to finish creating classes for the rest of our database, go ahead and map the rest of the database tables we created in *Chapter 2*. In case you need a refresher, take a look at the following screenshot:

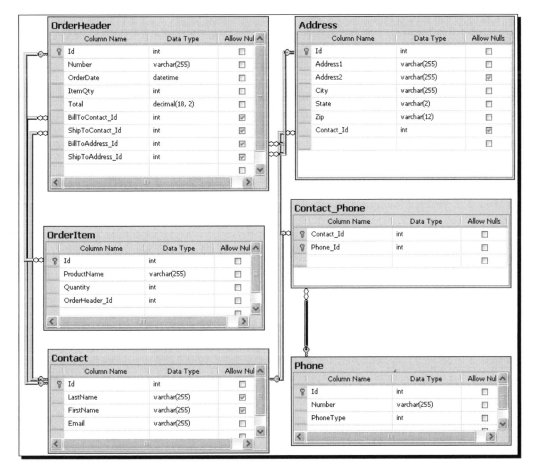

Pop quiz – mapping

1. How do we map a nullable integer from the database into our class?

    a. With an Integer (int or Integer)

    b. Nullable Integer (int? or Nullable(of Integer))

    c. This is not possible in .NET

    d. None of the above

2. How do we map associations (parent-child relationship) properties?

    a. Using value types (int or Integer)

    b. Using Generic types (IList<> or IList(of t))

    c. Using strings

3. How many constructors are required on a class?

    a. At least one

    b. None

    c. More than one

    d. The world may never know

Summary

We covered a lot of information in this chapter, mostly about mapping properties and default constructors.

Specifically, we covered:

◆ The use of constructors

◆ Creating public properties and private variables to hold our NHibernate data

◆ Converting SQL database types to CLR (.NET) types

◆ Creating properties to contain objects to represent Foreign Key fields

If you were able to map all of the tables we created in *Chapter 2*, then you are well on your way to becoming an NHibernate master!

Now that we've learned all about classes and datatypes, we're ready to dive into telling NHibernate HOW to actually map each field to the classes we have created, which is the topic of the next chapter.

4
Data Cartography

*Our next major hurdle in the implementation of NHibernate is database
mapping. In the last few chapters, we learned how to create tables to hold our
data and how to create classes to hold that data in our application. Now we
need to create the glue to bring them together.*

In this chapter, we will discuss:

- Different styles of mapping
- Mapping relationships
- Ways to load our objects
- Creating a database from our mapping files

Let's jump right in.

What is mapping?

Simply put, we need to tell NHibernate about the database that we created and how
the fields and tables match up to the properties and classes we created. We need to tell
NHibernate how we will be assigning Primary Keys, the data types that we will be using to
represent data, what variables we will store them in, and so on. You could say this is one
of the most important exercises we will perform in our pursuit of NHibernate. Don't worry
though, it's pretty easy.

Types of mapping

There are two basic ways to map data for NHibernate: the traditional XML mapping in an `hbm.xml` file, or the newer "Fluent NHibernate" style, which is similar to the interface pattern introduced with the .NET 3.5 framework (see `http://www.martinfowler.com/bliki/FluentInterface.html`).

In both cases, we will create a document for each of our tables. We will map each field from our database to the property we created to display it in our class.

XML mapping

XML mapping is undoubtedly the most common method of mapping entities with NHibernate. Basically, we create an XML document that contains all of the information about our classes and how it maps to our database tables.

These documents have several advantages:

- They are text files, so they are small
- They are very readable
- They use a very small number of tags to describe the data

The two biggest complaints about XML mapping is the verbosity of the text and that it is not compiled.

We can handle some of the verbosity by limiting the amount of data we put into the document. There are a number of optional parameters that do not absolutely need to be mapped, but that provide additional information about the database that can be included. We'll discuss more about that in the *Properties* section.

 You should copy the `nhibernate-mapping.xsd` and `nhibernate-configuration.xsd` files from the NHibernate ZIP file into your Visual Studio schemas directory (that is `C:\Program Files\Microsoft Visual Studio 9.0\Common7\Packages\schemas\xml`). This will give you IntelliSense and validation in the .NET XML editor when editing NHibernate mapping and configuration files.

Without compilation, when the database changes or the classes change, it's difficult to detect mismatches until the application is actually executed and NHibernate tries to reconcile the database structure with the mapping classes. While this can be an issue there are a number of ways to mitigate it, such as careful monitoring of changes, writing tests for our persistence layer, using a Visual Studio plugin, or using a code generation tool (we will learn more about this in *Chapter 11, It's a Generation Thing*).

Getting started

The XML mapping document begins like any XML document, with an XML declaration. No magic here, just a simple `xml` tag, and two attributes, `version` and `encoding`.

```
<?xml version="1.0" encoding="utf-8" ?>
```

The next tag we are going to see in our document is the `hibernate-mapping` tag. This tag has an attribute named `xmlns`, which is the XML namespace that the NHibernate mapping file should be validated against. This is directly related to a version of NHibernate, as each version has its own XML namespace to cover changes in the mapping language.

We can also use this tag to define the `namespace` and `assembly` that the class we are mapping resides in. The opening and closing tags for the `hibernate-mapping` tag are as shown in the following code snippet:

```
<hibernate-mapping xmlns="urn:nhibernate-mapping-2.2"
    namespace="BasicWebApplication.Common.DataObjects"
    assembly="BasicWebApplication">

</hibernate-mapping>
```

These three properties within the `hibernate-mapping` tag make up the basic XML mapping document.

Classes

The next tag we need to define in our document is the `class` tag. This is a KEY tag, because it tells NHibernate two things—the class this mapping document is meant to represent and which table in the database that class should map to.

The `class` tag has two attributes we need to be concerned with—`name` and `table`.

```
<class name="" table="">

</class>
```

The `name` attribute contains the fully-qualified POCO (or VB.NET) class that we want to map to, including the assembly name.

> While this can be specified in the standard fully-qualified dotted class name, a comma, and then the assembly name, the preferred method is to define the namespace and assembly in the `<hibernate-mapping>` tag, as shown in the previous code.

The `table` attribute specifies the table in the database that this mapping file represents. It can be as simple as the name of the table `Address` or as complex as needed to adequately describe the table.

If you need to include the owner of the table, such as `dbo.Address`, then you can add the `schema` attribute as follows:

```
schema="dbo"
```

If we were going to map the `Address` class in our application to the `Address` table in the database, then we would use a tag as follows:

```
<class name="Address" table="Address">

</class>
```

 Technically, as the table name is the same as our class name, we could leave out the `table` attribute.

Properties

We can map properties from our class to fields in the database using the `id` tag and the `property` tag. These tags are for the standard fields in the database, not the Foreign Key fields. We'll get to those in a minute.

The `id` and `property` tags follow a standard pattern and have a number of optional parameters. They follow the basic format of defining the property on the class that they are mapping to and the data type that is used to represent that data. This will generally look as follows:

```
<property name="Address1" type="String">
  <column name="Address1" length="255" sql-type="varchar"
      not-null="true"/>
</property>
```

This is the fully-verbose method of mapping the properties, and the one I personally use. If something happens to your database, you can re-generate the database from this information. It's also very helpful when you are troubleshooting because all of the information about the data is right there.

Alternately, you can map the property as follows:

```
<property name="Address1" />
```

Both methods will provide the same mapping to NHibernate, but as I stated earlier, the more verbose method gives you a lot more flexibility.

One of the optional attributes that I generally use on the id and property tags is the type attribute. With this attribute I can tell NHibernate that I am using a particular type of data to store that information in my class. Adding this data type, our property tag would look as follows:

```
<property name="Address1" type="String" />
```

I also like to use the column tag, just to explicitly link the field with the property in the class, but that again is just preference. The previous code is completely adequate.

ID columns

The first property from our class that we want to map is the Id property. This tag has a number of attributes we can optionally set, but the simplest way we can map the Id property is as follows:

```
<id name="Id">
  <generator class="hilo"/>
</id>
```

This tells NHibernate that we have a property in our class named Id which maps to a field in the database called Id and also that we use the hilo method to automatically generate a value for this field. Simple enough!

An optional attribute that I generally use on the id tag is the unsaved-value attribute. This attribute specifies what value should be returned in a new object before it is persisted (saved) to the database. Adding this attribute, as well as the type attribute we talked about, the code would look as follows:

```
<id name="Id" type="Int32" unsaved-value="null">
  <generator class="hilo"/>
</id>
```

As long as our field is named Id in the database, we are good to go. But what if it was named id or address_id? This simply wouldn't handle it. In that case, we would have to add the optional column tag to identify it:

```
<id name="Id">
  <column name="address_id"/>
  <generator class="hilo"/>
</id>
```

Now we have mapped our `address_id` field from the database into a more standard `Id` property on our class. Some of the additional attributes that are commonly used on the `column` tag are as follows:

- ◆ `name`: Define the name of the column in the database
- ◆ `length`: The length of the field, as defined in the database
- ◆ `sql-type`: The database definition of the column type
- ◆ `not-null`: Whether or not the database column allows nulls. `not-null="true"` specifies a required field

Again, these optional attributes simply allow you to further define how your database is created. Some people don't even define the database. They just define the `hbm.xml` files and use the `NHibernate.Tool.hbm2ddl` to create a SQL script to do this work! We'll talk more about this in *Chapter 12, Odds and Ends*.

Mapping our types

Let's take a few minutes and map the basic fields from the `OrderHeader` table we created earlier. What we really need to do is map all of the "standard" fields (`ints`, `varchars`, `datetimes`, `decimals`, and so on) to their .NET counterparts we created in the classes in *Chapter 3, A touch of class*.

Time for action – mapping basic types

Take a look at the following **OrderHeader** table. We need to map the **Number**, **OrderDate**, **ItemQty**, and **Total** fields into our `OrderHeader` class.

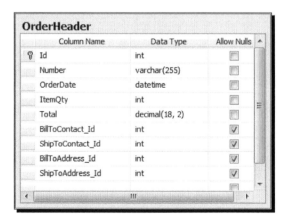

OrderHeader		
Column Name	Data Type	Allow Nulls
🔑 Id	int	☐
Number	varchar(255)	☐
OrderDate	datetime	☐
ItemQty	int	☐
Total	decimal(18, 2)	☐
BillToContact_Id	int	☑
ShipToContact_Id	int	☑
BillToAddress_Id	int	☑
ShipToAddress_Id	int	☑

1. Open the `OrderHeader` class we created in *Chapter 3*. This will be either
`OrderHeader.cs` or `OrderHeader.vb`. We will use this file for reference
while we create our mapping document. Your class should look as follows:

```
using System;
using System.Collections.Generic;
using System.Text;

namespace Ordering.Data
{
  public class OrderHeader
  {
    #region Constructors

      public OrderHeader() { }

      public OrderHeader(string Number, DateTime OrderDate,
          int ItemQty, decimal Total, Contact BillToContact,
          Contact ShipToContact, Address BillToAddress,
          Address ShipToAddress): this()
      {
        this.Number = Number;
        this.OrderDate = OrderDate;
        this.ItemQty = ItemQty;
        this.Total = Total;
        this.BillToContact = BillToContact;
        this.ShipToContact = ShipToContact;
        this.BillToAddress = BillToAddress;
        this.ShipToAddress = ShipToAddress;
      }

    #endregion

    #region Properties

      private int _id;
      public virtual int Id
      {
        get { return _id; }
        set { _id = value; }
      }

      private string _number;
      public virtual string Number
      {
```

```
    get { return _number; }
    set { _number = value; }
  }

  private DateTime _orderDate;
  public virtual DateTime OrderDate
  {
    get { return _orderDate; }
    set { _orderDate = value; }
  }

  private int _itemQty;
  public virtual int ItemQty
  {
    get { return _itemQty; }
    set { _itemQty = value; }
  }

  private decimal _total;
  public virtual decimal Total
  {
    get { return _total; }
    set { _total = value; }
  }

  private IList<OrderItem> _orderItems;
  public virtual IList<OrderItem> OrderItems
  {
    get { return _orderItems; }
    set { _orderItems = value; }
  }

  private Contact _billToContact;
  public virtual Contact BillToContact
  {
    get { return _billToContact; }
    set { _billToContact = value; }
  }

  private Contact _shipToContact;
  public virtual Contact ShipToContact
  {
    get { return _shipToContact; }
    set { _shipToContact = value; }
```

```
        }

        private Address _billToAddress;
        public virtual Address BillToAddress
        {
          get { return _billToAddress; }
          set { _billToAddress = value; }
        }

        private Address _shipToAddress;
        public virtual Address ShipToAddress
        {
          get { return _shipToAddress; }
          set { _shipToAddress = value; }
        }

    #endregion
  }
}
```

Or in VB.NET, it will look as follows:

```
Public Class OrderHeader

#Region "Constructors"
  Public Sub New()
  End Sub

  Public Sub New(ByVal Number As String, ByVal OrderDate As _
              DateTime, ByVal ItemQty As Integer, ByVal Total _
              As Decimal, ByVal BillToContact As Contact, _
              ByVal ShipToContact As Contact, ByVal _
              BillToAddress As Address, ByVal ShipToAddress _
              As Address)
    Me.New()
    Me.Number = Number
    Me.OrderDate = OrderDate
    Me.ItemQty = ItemQty
    Me.Total = Total
    Me.BillToContact = BillToContact
    Me.ShipToContact = ShipToContact
    Me.BillToAddress = BillToAddress
    Me.ShipToAddress = ShipToAddress
  End Sub

#End Region
```

```vbnet
#Region "Properties"
  Private _id As Integer
    Public Overridable Property Id() As Integer
      Get
        Return _id
      End Get
      Set(ByVal value As Integer)
        _id = value
      End Set
    End Property

    Private _number As String
    Public Overridable Property Number() As String
      Get
        Return _number
      End Get
      Set(ByVal value As String)
        _number = value
      End Set
    End Property

    Private _orderDate As DateTime
    Public Overridable Property OrderDate() As DateTime
      Get
        Return _orderDate
      End Get
      Set(ByVal value As DateTime)
        _orderDate = value
      End Set
    End Property

    Private _itemQty As Integer
    Public Overridable Property ItemQty() As Integer
      Get
        Return _itemQty
      End Get
      Set(ByVal value As Integer)
        _itemQty = value
      End Set
    End Property

    Private _total As Decimal
    Public Overridable Property Total() As Decimal
      Get
```

```vbnet
      Return _total
    End Get
    Set(ByVal value As Decimal)
      _total = value
    End Set
End Property


Private _orderItems As IList(Of OrderItem)
Public Overridable Property OrderItems() As IList_
  (Of OrderItem)
    Get
      Return _orderItems
    End Get
    Set(ByVal value As IList(Of OrderItem))
      _orderItems = value
    End Set
End Property


Private _billToContact As Contact
Public Overridable Property BillToContact() As Contact
    Get
      Return _billToContact
    End Get
    Set(ByVal value As Contact)
      _billToContact = value
    End Set
End Property


Private _shipToContact As Contact
Public Overridable Property ShipToContact() As Contact
    Get
      Return _shipToContact
    End Get
    Set(ByVal value As Contact)
      _shipToContact = value
    End Set
End Property


Private _billToAddress As Address
Public Overridable Property BillToAddress() As Address
    Get
      Return _billToAddress
    End Get
    Set(ByVal value As Address)
```

```
          _billToAddress = value
      End Set
    End Property


    Private _shipToAddress As Address
    Public Overridable Property ShipToAddress() As Address
      Get
        Return _shipToAddress
      End Get
      Set(ByVal value As Address)
        _shipToAddress = value
      End Set
    End Property
#End Region
End Class
```

2. Before we get started, let's create a few folders to make our job a little easier. Right-click on your **Ordering.Data** project and click on **Add | New Folder**.

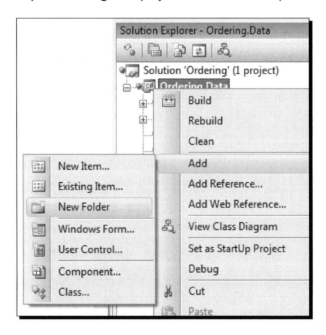

3. Let's name the folder **Common**, and we'll drag all of our existing classes (`Address`, `Contact`, `OrderHeader`, and `OrderItem`) into that folder. This will make it easier to find things as we get more files.

4. Using the same procedure, create a new folder called **Mapping** so we can add our `hbm.xml` mapping files. When you are done, it should look as follows:

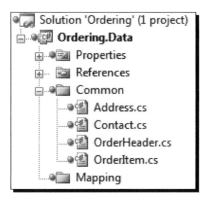

5. Right-click on the **Mapping** folder and click **Add | New Item**.

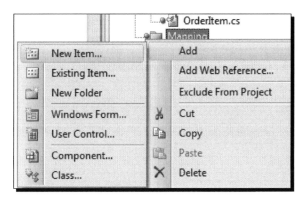

6. In the **Add New Item – Ordering.Data** dialog box, select **Data** as the category, then **XML File** under the template. Name the template **OrderHeader.hbm.xml** and click on **Add**.

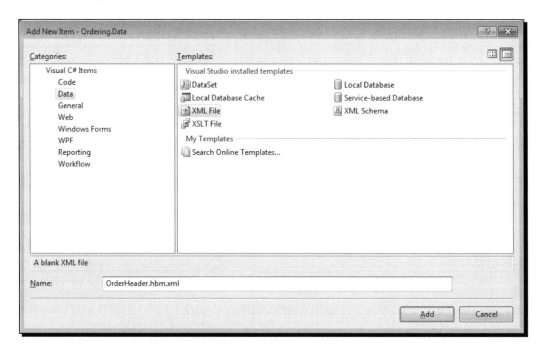

7. Once the new file has been created, it will open in the editor. It should look something like the following screenshot:

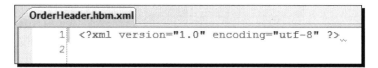

8. The first thing we want to do with our mapping file is to ensure that it gets compiled into our assembly so NHibernate can find it. Right-click on the **OrderHeader.hbm.xml** file and select **Properties**.

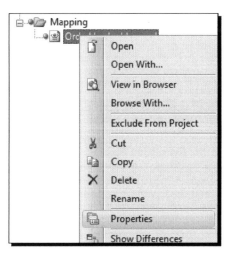

9. In the **Properties** dialog, drop down the **Build Auction** menu and select **Embedded Resource**. This will ensure that the file is compiled into our assembly.

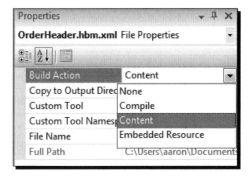

10. Inside our `OrderHeader.hbm.xml` document, we want to add the actual mapping data. The first thing we need to add is our `nhibernate-mapping` element. This will become the root element for our document. Under the `<?xml version="1.0" encoding="utf-8" ?>` tag, add the `hibernate-mapping` tags. Your document should look as follows:

```
<?xml version="1.0" encoding="utf-8" ?>
<hibernate-mapping xmlns="urn:nhibernate-mapping-2.2"
  namespace="Ordering.Data.OrderHeader",
  assembly="Ordering.Data">
</hibernate-mapping>
```

11. The next element that we will need in our mapping document is the `class` element. This element lets NHibernate know which class in our assembly maps to which table in the database. Add a `class` tag to map the `OrderHeader` class to the OrderHeader table as follows:

```
<?xml version="1.0" encoding="utf-8" ?>
<hibernate-mapping xmlns="urn:nhibernate-mapping-2.2">
  <class name=" OrderHeader" table="OrderHeader">
  </class>
</hibernate-mapping>
```

12. Now, we need to map our `Id` field. Between the opening and closing `class` tags, add the following code to map our `Id` field, and let NHibernate know that it's an `Identity` field by using the native `generator` class:

```
<class name=" OrderHeader " table="OrderHeader">
  <id name="Id">
    <generator class="hilo"/>
  </id>
</class>
```

13. If you wish, you can also map the field with all the data required to generate the database, as follows:

```
<id name="Id" type="Int32" unsaved-value="null">
  <column name="Id" length="4" sql-type="int" not-null="true"
      unique="true" index="PK_OrderHeader"/>
  <generator class="hilo" />
</id>
```

 Most programmers opt for the first syntax when they are handcoding, as it is much less to type! However, when I automatically generate these XML documents with a code generator, I opt to include the additional information to help me troubleshoot later (should something go wrong).

14. Next, we need to map our remaining properties into the `class` element. Add the `Number`, `OrderDate`, `ItemQty`, and `Total` properties as follows:

```
<property name="Number" type="String"/>
<property name="OrderDate" type="DateTime"/>
<property name="ItemQty" type="Int32"/>
<property name="Total" type="Decimal"/>
```

15. That should do it! Your `OrderHeader.hbm.xml` file should look as follows:

```xml
<?xml version="1.0" encoding="utf-8" ?>
<hibernate-mapping xmlns="urn:nhibernate-mapping-2.2">
  <class name="Ordering.Data.OrderHeader, Ordering.Data"
      table="OrderHeader">
    <id name="Id">
    <column name="Id"/>
    <generator class="native"/>
    </id>
    <property name="Number" type="String"/>
    <property name="OrderDate" type="DateTime"/>
    <property name="ItemQty" type="Int32"/>
    <property name="Total" type="Decimal"/>
  </class>
</hibernate-mapping>
```

What just happened?

We created an `hbm.xml` mapping file for our `OrderHeader` table and included all of the non-Foreign Key fields. By mapping all of the fields, NHibernate now understands which fields from the database we are using in our classes.

Pop quiz – class mapping

1. What attributes are required on the `property` tag?

    a. `type`

    b. `name`

    c. `column`

    d. `name` and `type`

2. Which of the following is a correct `class` implementation?

    a. `<class type="MyNamespace.MyClass, MyAssembly">`

    b. `<class mapping_table="MyTable">`

    c. `<class type="MyAssembly " table="MyTable">`

    d. `<class name="MyAssembly" table="MyTable">`

Relationships

Remember all those great relationships we created in our database to relate our tables together? If you need a refresher, then head back over to the *Relationships* section of *Chapter 2, Database Layout and Design*. Basically, the primary types of relationships are as follows:

- **One-to-many (OTM)**
- **Many-to-one (MTO)**
- **One-to-one (OTO)**
- **Many-to-many (MTM)**

We won't focus on the OTO relationship because it is really uncommon. In most situations, if there is a need for a one-to-one relationship, it should probably be consolidated into the main table.

One-to-many relationships

The most common type of relationship we will map is a one-to-many (OTM) and the other way—many-to-one (MTO). If you remember, these are just two different sides of the same relationship, as seen in the following screenshot:

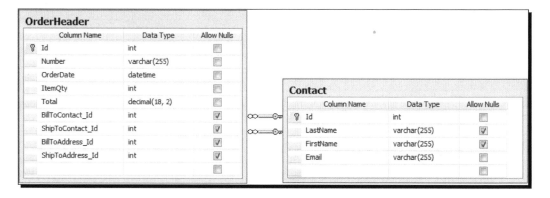

This is a simple one-to-many (OTM) relationship where a **Contact** can be associated with zero to many **OrderHeader** records (because the relationship fields allow nulls). Notice that the Foreign Key for the relationship is stored on the "many" side, **ShipToContact_Id** and **BillToContact_Id** on the **OrderHeader** table. In our mapping files, we can map this relationship from both sides.

If you remember, our classes for these objects contain placeholders for each side of this relationship. On the `OrderHeader` side, we have a `Contact` object called `BillToContact`:

```
private Contact _billToContact;
public Contact BillToContact
{
  get { return _billToContact; }
  set { _billToContact = value; }
}
```

On the Contact side, we have the inverse relationship mapped. From this vantage point, there could be SEVERAL `OrderHeaders` objects that this `Contact` object is associated with, so we needed a collection to map it:

```
private IList<OrderHeader> _billTOrderHeaders;
public IList<OrderHeader> BillTOrderHeaders
{
  get { return _billTOrderHeaders; }
  set { _billTOrderHeaders = value; }
}
```

As we have mapped this collection in two separate classes, we also need to map it in two separate mapping files. Let's start with the `OrderHeader` side. As this is the "many" side of the one-to-many relationship, we need to use a many-to-one type to map it. Things to note here are the `name` and `class` attributes. `name`, again, is the property in our class that this field maps to, and `class` is the "other end" of the Foreign Key relationship or the `Contact` type in this case.

```
<many-to-one name="BillToContact" class="Contact">
  <column name="BillToContact_Id" length="4" sql-type="int"
      not-null="false"/>
</many-to-one>
```

Just like before, when we mapped our non-relational fields, the `length`, `sql-type`, and `not-null` attributes are optional.

Now that we have the "one" side mapped, we need to map the "many" side. In the `contact` mapping file, we need to create a `bag` element to hold all of these `OrderHeaders`. A bag is the NHibernate way to say that it is an unordered collection allowing duplicated items. We have a `name` element to reference the `class` property just like all of our other mapping elements and a `key` child element to tell NHibernate which database column this field is meant to represent.

```
<bag name="BillToOrderHeaders" inverse="true
    cascade="all-delete-orphan">
  <key column="BillToContact_Id"/>
  <one-to-many
    class="BasicWebApplication.Common.DataObjects.OrderHeader,
      BasicWebApplication"/>
</bag>
```

If you look at the previous XML code, you will see that the `one-to-many` tag looks very similar to the `many-to-one` tag we just created for the other side. That's because this is the inverse side of the relationship. We even tell NHibernate that the inverse relationship exists by using the `inverse` attribute on the `bag` element. The `class` attribute on this tag is just the name of the class that represents the other side of the relationship.

The `cascade` attribute tells NHibernate how to handle objects when we delete them. Another attribute we can add to the bag tag is the `lazy` attribute. This tells NHibernate to use "lazy loading", which means that the record won't be pulled from the database or loaded into memory until you actually use it. This is a huge performance gain because you only get data when you need it, without having to do anything. When I say "get `Contact` record with Id 14", NHibernate will go get the `Contact` record, but it won't retrieve the associated `BillToOrderHeaders` (OrderHeader records) until I reference `Contact`. `BillToOrderHeaders` to display or act on those objects in my code. By default, "lazy loading" is turned on, so we only need to specify this tag if we want to turn "lazy loading" off by using `lazy="false"`.

Many-to-many relationships

The other relationship that is used quite often is the many-to -many (MTM) relationship. In the following example, the **Contact_Phone** table is used to join the **Contact** and **Phone** tables. NHibernate is smart enough to manage these MTM relationships for us, and we can "optimize out" the join table from our classes and just let NHibernate take care of it.

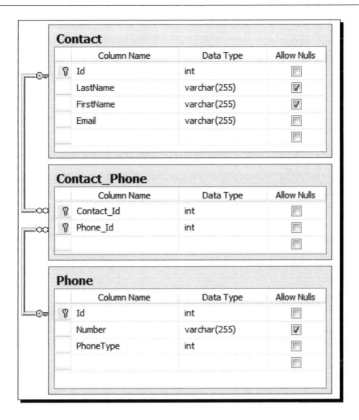

Just like the one-to-many relationship, we represent the phones on the `Contact` class with a collection of `Phone` objects as follows:

```
private IList<Phone> _phones;
public IList<Phone> Phones
{
  get { return _ phones; }
  set { _ phones = value; }
}
```

Mapping the MTM is very similar to the OTM, just a little more complex. We still use a bag and we still have a key. We need to add the table attribute to the bag element to let NHibernate know which table we are really storing the relationship data in. Instead of a one-to-many and a many-to-one attribute, both sides use a many-to-many element (makes sense, it is an MTM relationship, right?). The many-to-many element structure is the same as the one-to-many element, with a class attribute and a column child element to describe the relationship.

```
<bag name="Phones" table="Contact_Phone" inverse="false" lazy="true"
    cascade="none">
  <key>
    <column name="Contact_Id" length="4" sql-type="int"
      not-null="true"/>
  </key>
  <many-to-many class=" Phone">
    <column name="Phone_Id" length="4" sql-type="int"
      not-null="true"/>
  </many-to-many>
</bag>
```

From the Phone side, it looks remarkably similar, as it's just the opposite view of the same relationship:

```
<bag name="Contacts" table="Contact_Phone" inverse="false"
    lazy="true" cascade="none">
  <key>
    <column name="Phone_Id" length="4" sql-type="int"
      not-null="true"/>
  </key>
  <many-to-many class=" Contact ">
    <column name="Contact_Id" length="4" sql-type="int"
      not-null="true"/>
  </many-to-many>
</bag>
```

Getting started

This should be enough information to get us rolling on the path to becoming NHibernate superstars! Now that we have all of the primary fields mapped, let's map the Foreign Key fields.

Time for action – mapping relationships

If you look at the following database diagram, you will see that there are two relationships that need to be mapped, `BillToContact` and `ShipToContact` (represented by **BillToContact_Id** and **ShipToContact_Id** in the following screenshot).

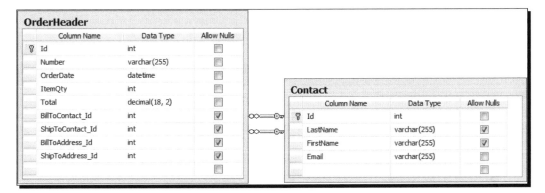

Let's map these two properties into our `hbm.xml` files.

1. Open the `OrderHeader.hbm.xml` file, which should look something as follows:

```xml
<?xml version="1.0" encoding="utf-8" ?>
<hibernate-mapping xmlns="urn:nhibernate-mapping-2.2"
        namespace="Ordering.Data" assembly="Ordering.Data">
  <class name="OrderHeader" table="OrderHeader ">
    <id name="Id">
      <column name="Id"/>
      <generator class="hilo"/>
    </id>
    <property name="Number" type="String"/>
    <property name="OrderDate" type="DateTime"/>
    <property name="ItemQty" type="Int32"/>
    <property name="Total" type="Decimal"/>
  </class>
</hibernate-mapping>
```

2. After the `Total` property, just before the end of the `class` tag (`</class>`), add a `many-to-one` element to map the `BillToContact` to the `Contact` class.

```xml
<many-to-one name="BillToContact" class="Ordering.Data.Contact,
        Ordering.Data">
  <column name="BillToContact_Id" />
</many-to-one>
```

3. Next, open the `Contact.hbm.xml` file, which should look as follows:

```xml
<?xml version="1.0" encoding="utf-8" ?>
<hibernate-mapping xmlns="urn:nhibernate-mapping-2.2"
    namespace="Ordering.Data" assembly="Ordering.Data">
  <class name=" Contact " table="Contact">
    <id name="Id">
      <column name="Id"/>
      <generator class="hilo"/>
    </id>
    <property name="FirstName" type="String"/>
    <property name="LastName" type="String"/>
    <property name="Email" type="String"/>
  </class>
</hibernate-mapping>
```

4. After the `Email` property, just before the end of the `class` tag (`</class>`), add a `one-to-many` element to map the `BillToOrderHeaders` to the `OrderHeader` class.

```xml
<bag name="BillToOrderHeaders" inverse="true" lazy="true"
    cascade="all-delete-orphan">
  <key column="BillToContact_Id"/>
  <one-to-many class="OrderHeader "/>
</bag>
```

5. That's it! You just mapped your first one-to-many property! Your finished `Contact.hbm.xml` class should look as shown in the following screenshot:

```
 1   <?xml version="1.0" encoding="utf-8" ?>
 2   <hibernate-mapping xmlns="urn:nhibernate-mapping-2.2"
 3     namespace="Ordering.Data" assembly="Ordering.Data">
 4     <class name="Contact " table="Contact">
 5       <id name="Id">
 6         <column name="Id"/>
 7         <generator class="hilo"/>
 8       </id>
 9       <property name="FirstName" type="String"/>
10       <property name="LastName" type="String"/>
11       <property name="Email" type="String"/>
12       <bag name="BillToOrderHeaders" inverse="true"
13           lazy="true" cascade="all-delete-orphan">
14         <key column="BillToContact_Id"/>
15         <one-to-many class="OrderHeader"/>
16       </bag>
17     </class>
18   </hibernate-mapping>
```

What just happened?

By adding `one-to-many` and `many-to-one` child elements to the `bag` tag, we were able to map the relationships to the `Contact` object, allowing us to use dotted notation to access child properties of our objects within our code.

Like the great cartographers before us, we have the knowledge and experience to go forth and map the world!

Have a go hero – flushing out the rest of our map

Now that you have some experience mapping fields and Foreign Keys from the database, why not have a go at the rest of our database! Start off with the Contact-to-Phone MTM table, and map the rest of the tables to the classes we created earlier, so that we will be ready to actually connect to the database in the next chapter!

Fluent mapping

While XML mapping is undoubtedly the most common mapping method, the fluent NHibernate method is gaining steam. This is a separate project from the main NHibernate project, and you can find out more information about it at `http://fluentnhibernate.org/`.

Some of the advantages of fluent mapping over XML mapping are as follows:

◆ **Compile-time mapping validation**: XML is not evaluated by the compiler, so renaming properties in your classes or other errors in your `hbm.xml` mapping would not be detected until you actually run the application

◆ **Less verbose**: XML by nature is fairly easy to read because of the number of characters it requires to produce even simple documents, but this makes for huge documents

◆ **Fewer repetitions**: Instead of writing the same repetitive XML over and over, the fluent interface exposes the advantages of native code

Fluent NHibernate provides these advantages by moving your mappings from XML documents directly into your code. They're compiled along with your application! You can also use Fluent's configuration system to specify patterns to make your code simpler and more readable.

Remember the `Address` table we created for our Ordering system, shown in the following screenshot? Let's take a look at a fluent map for this table.

	Column Name	Data Type	Allow Nulls
🔑	Id	int	☐
	Address1	varchar(255)	☐
	Address2	varchar(255)	☑
	City	varchar(255)	☐
	State	varchar(2)	☐
	Zip	varchar(12)	☐
	Contact_Id	int	☑
▶			☐

The traditional XML map for this table would look something like the following block of code:

```xml
<?xml version="1.0" encoding="utf-8" ?>
<hibernate-mapping xmlns="urn:nhibernate-mapping-2.2">
  <class name="BasicWebApplication.Common.DataObjects.Address,
      BasicWebApplication" table="Address">
    <id name="Id" type="Int32" unsaved-value="null">
      <column name="Id" length="4" sql-type="int" not-null="true"
          unique="true" index="PK_Address"/>
      <generator class="hilo" />
    </id>
    <property name="Address1" type="String">
      <column name="Address1" length="255" sql-type="varchar"
          not-null="true"/>
    </property>
    <property name="Address2" type="String">
      <column name="Address2" length="255" sql-type="varchar"
          not-null="false"/>
    </property>
    <property name="City" type="String">
      <column name="City" length="255" sql-type="varchar"
          not-null="true"/>
    </property>
    <property name="State" type="String">
      <column name="`State`" length="2" sql-type="varchar"
          not-null="true"/>
    </property>
    <property name="Zip" type="String">
      <column name="Zip" length="12" sql-type="varchar"
          not-null="true"/>
    </property>
```

```
<many-to-one name="Contact"
    class="BasicWebApplication.Common.DataObjects.Contact,
    BasicWebApplication">
  <column name="Contact_Id" length="4" sql-type="int"
    not-null="false"/>
</many-to-one>
<bag name="BillToOrderHeaders" inverse="true" lazy="true"
    cascade="all-delete-orphan">
  <key column="BillToAddress_Id"/>
  <one-to-many class="BasicWebApplication.Common.DataObjects.
    OrderHeader, BasicWebApplication"/>
</bag>
<bag name="ShipToOrderHeaders" inverse="true" lazy="true"
    cascade="all-delete-orphan">
  <key column="ShipToAddress_Id"/>
  <one-to-many class="BasicWebApplication.Common.DataObjects.
    OrderHeader, BasicWebApplication"/>
</bag>
</class>
</hibernate-mapping>
```

You have to admit that the code is pretty readable, but it sure is verbose! Do I really need 35 lines of code to describe classes that are already contained in my application? Wouldn't it be cleaner to just write it as follows?

```
public class AddressMap : ClassMap<Address>
{
  WithTable("Address");
  Id(x => x.Id);
  Map(x => x.Address1).WithLengthOf(255);
  Map(x => x.Address2).WithLengthOf(255).Nullable();
  Map(x => x.City).WithLengthOf(255);
  Map(x => x.State).WithLengthOf(2);
  Map(x => x.Zip).WithLengthOf(12);
  References(x => x. Contact).Nullable();
  HasMany(x => x.BillToOrderHeaders).Inverse().Cascade.All();
  HasMany(x => x.ShipToOrderHeaders).Inverse().Cascade.All();
}
```

The preceding code is definitely more readable, if only because it's shorter.

The advantages of the fluent interface are many, from simpler compiled code to being able to fit the entire table mapping onto one page.

If you are looking for an even simpler method, and if you can follow a couple of simple conventions when you create your database, then you can use the "Auto Persistence Model" to automatically map your data, and you don't need to write any mapping code at all! This method is perfect if you have control of your database structure (you are the database administrator or at least can change field names in the database if you want them changed in your classes). All you have to do is create your tables, create your object classes (POCOs), and tell Fluent to auto-map the tables to the classes because they have the same name.

Better yet, just create your POCOs, and use NHibernate to generate your database and Fluent NHibernate to map it!

Pop quiz – fluent mapping

1. Which of the following is an advantage of fluent mapping?

   a. More verbose

   b. Integrated e-mail support

   c. Compile-time mapping validation

   d. None of the above

2. Fluent can be used without writing a single line of mapping code.

   a. True

   b. False

   c. Using Strings

Summary

Wow, we made a lot of progress in this chapter! We talked more about mapping in a few pages than most people learn in a lifetime.

Specifically, we covered:

- How to map the basic elements of a table into a class
- Mapping OTM and MTM relationships
- The basics of Fluent mapping

Now that we're NHibernate mapping rockstars, we're ready to talk about connecting to the database and managing NHibernate sessions, which is the topic of the next chapter.

5
The Session Procession

Using what we have already learned, NHibernate knows enough about our data structure and our objects. Now it's time to let NHibernate connect to the database.

In this chapter, we'll talk about:

- What is an NHibernate session?
- How does it differ from a regular database session?
- Retrieving and committing data
- Session strategies for ASP.NET

Using what we have already learned and the information in this chapter, we will be able to store and retrieve information from the database!

What is an NHibernate session?

Think of an NHibernate session as an abstract or virtual conduit to the database. Gone are the days when you have to create a `Connection`, open the `Connection`, pass the `Connection` to a `Command` object, create a `DataReader` from the `Command` object, and so on.

With NHibernate, we ask the `SessionFactory` for a `Session` object, and that's it. NHibernate handles all of the "real" sessions to the database, connections, pooling, and so on. We reap all the benefits without having to know the underlying intricacies of all of the database backends we are trying to connect to.

Time for action – getting ready

Before we actually connect to the database, we need to do a little "housekeeping". Just a note, if you run into trouble (that is, your code doesn't work like the walkthrough), then don't panic. See the troubleshooting section at the end of this *Time for action* section.

1. Before we get started, make sure that you have all of the Mapping and Common files and that your Mapping files are included as "Embedded Resources" (if you're not sure, see *Chapter 4, Data Cartography*). Your project should look as shown in the following screenshot:

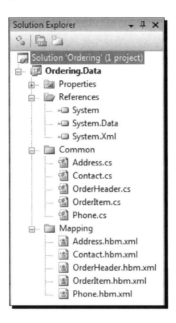

2. The first thing we need to do is create a new project to use to create our sessions. Right-click on the **Solution 'Ordering'** and click on **Add | New Project**.

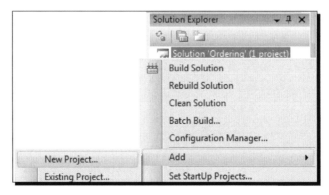

3. For our tests, we will use a **Console Application** and name it **Ordering.Console**. Use the same location as your previous project.

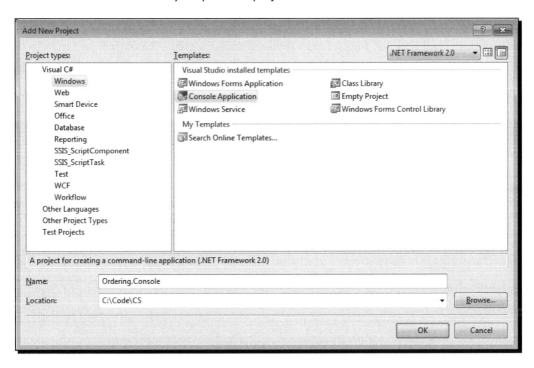

4. Next, we need to add a few references. Right-click on the **References** folder and click on **Add Reference**. In VB.NET, you need to right-click on the **Ordering.Console** project, and click on **Add Reference**.

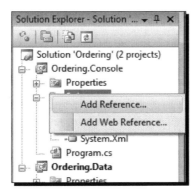

5. Select the **Browse** tab, and navigate to the folder that contains your NHibernate DLLs. You should have six files in this folder. Select the **NHibernate.dll**, **Castle.Core. dll**, **Castle.DynamicProxy2.dll**, **Iesi.Collections.dll**, **log4net.dll**, and **NHibernate. ByteCode.Castle.dll** files, and click on **OK** to add them as references to the project.

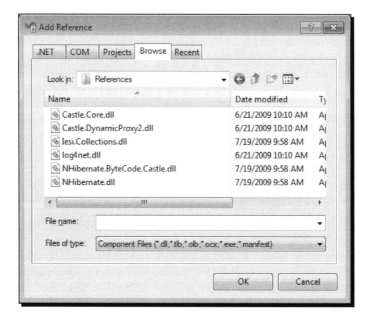

6. Right-click on the **References** folder (or the project folder in VB.NET), and click on **Add Reference** again. Select the **Projects** tab, select the **Ordering.Data** project, and click on **OK** to add the data tier as a reference to our console application.

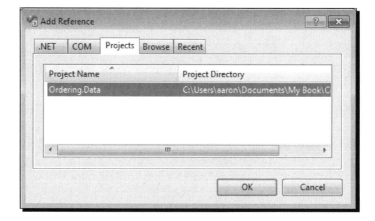

7. The last thing we need to do is create a configuration object. We will discuss configuration in a later chapter, so for now, it would suffice to say that this will give us everything we need to connect to the database. Your current `Program.cs` file in the `Ordering.Console` application should look as follows:

```
using System;
using System.Collections.Generic;
using System.Text;

namespace Ordering.Console
{
    class Program
    {
        static void Main(string[] args)
        {
        }
    }
}
```

Or, if you are using VB.NET, your `Module1.vb` file will look as follows:

```
Module Module1

    Sub Main()
    End Sub

End Module
```

8. At the top of the file, we need to import a few references to make our project compile. Right above the `namespace` or `Module` declarations, add the `using/Imports` statements for `NHibernate`, `NHibernate.Cfg`, and `Ordering.Data`:

```
using NHibernate;
using NHibernate.Cfg;
using Ordering.Data;
```

In VB.NET you need to use the `Imports` keyword as follows:

```
Imports NHibernate
Imports NHibernate.Cfg
Imports Ordering.Data
```

9. Inside the `Main()` block, we want to create the `configuration` object that will tell NHibernate how to connect to the database. Inside your `Main()` block, add the following code:

```
Configuration cfg = new Configuration();
cfg.Properties.Add(NHibernate.Cfg.Environment.ConnectionProvider,
    typeof(NHibernate.Connection.DriverConnectionProvider)
    .AssemblyQualifiedName);

cfg.Properties.Add(NHibernate.Cfg.Environment.Dialect,
    typeof(NHibernate.Dialect.MsSql2008Dialect)
    .AssemblyQualifiedName);

cfg.Properties.Add(NHibernate.Cfg.Environment.ConnectionDriver,
    typeof(NHibernate.Driver.SqlClientDriver)
    .AssemblyQualifiedName);

cfg.Properties.Add(NHibernate.Cfg.Environment.ConnectionString,
    "Server= (local)\\SQLExpress;Database=
    Ordering;Trusted_Connection=true;");

cfg.Properties.Add(NHibernate.Cfg.Environment.
    ProxyFactoryFactoryClass, typeof
    (NHibernate.ByteCode.LinFu.ProxyFactoryFactory)
    .AssemblyQualifiedName);


cfg.AddAssembly(typeof(Address).AssemblyQualifiedName);
```

For a VB.NET project, add the following code:

```
Dim cfg As New Configuration()
cfg.Properties.Add(NHibernate.Cfg.Environment. _
    ConnectionProvider, GetType(NHibernate.Connection. _
    DriverConnectionProvider).AssemblyQualifiedName)

cfg.Properties.Add(NHibernate.Cfg.Environment.Dialect, _
    GetType(NHibernate.Dialect.MsSql2008Dialect). _
    AssemblyQualifiedName)

cfg.Properties.Add(NHibernate.Cfg.Environment.ConnectionDriver, _
    GetType(NHibernate.Driver.SqlClientDriver). _
AssemblyQualifiedName)
```

```
cfg.Properties.Add(NHibernate.Cfg.Environment.ConnectionString, _
  "Server= (local)\SQLExpress;Database=Ordering; _
    Trusted_Connection=true;")

cfg.Properties.Add(NHibernate.Cfg.Environment. _
  ProxyFactoryFactoryClass, GetType _
  (NHibernate.ByteCode.LinFu.ProxyFactoryFactory). _
  AssemblyQualifiedName)

cfg.AddAssembly(GetType(Address).AssemblyQualifiedName)
```

10. Lastly, right-click on the **Ordering.Console** project, and select **Set as Startup Project**, as shown in the following screenshot:

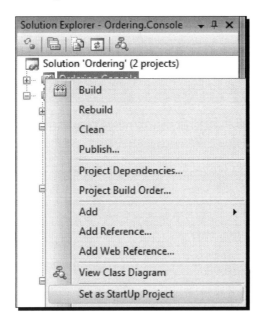

11. Press *F5* or **Debug | Start Debugging** and test your project. If everything goes well, you should see a command prompt window pop up and then go away. Congratulations! You are done!

12. However, it is more than likely you will get an error on the line that says `cfg.AddAssembly()`. This line instructs NHibernate to "take all of my `HBM.xml` files and compile them". This is where we will find out how well we handcoded our `HBM.xml` files.

The most common error that will show up is **MappingException was unhandled**. If you get a mapping exception, then see the next step for troubleshooting tips.

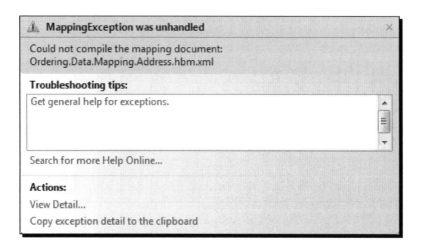

13. **Troubleshooting:** NHibernate will tell us where the errors are and why they are an issue. The first step to debug these issues is to click on the **View Detail** link under **Actions** on the error pop up. This will bring up the **View Detail** dialog, as shown in the following screenshot:

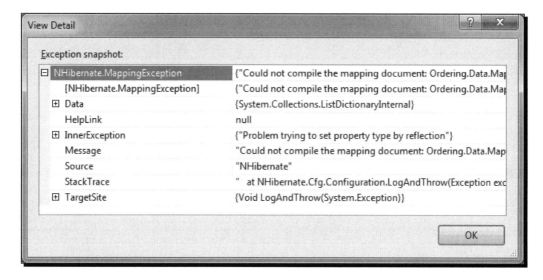

14. If you look at the message, NHibernate says that it **Could not compile the mapping document: Ordering.Data.Mapping.Address.hbm.xml**. So now we know that the issue is in our `Address.hbm.xml` file, but this is not very helpful. If we look at the **InnerException**, it says **"Problem trying to set property type by reflection"**. Still not a specific issue, but if we click on the **+** next to the **InnerException**, I can see that there is an **InnerException** on this exception.

The second **InnerException** says **"class Ordering.Data.Address, Ordering.Data, Version=1.0.0.0, Culture=neutral, PublicKeyToken=null not found while looking for property: Id"**.

Now we are getting closer. It has something to do with the ID property. But wait, there is another **InnerException**. This **InnerException** says **"Could not find a getter for property 'Id' in class 'Ordering.Data.Address'"**. How could that be? Looking at my `Address.cs` class, I see:

```
using System;
using System.Collections.Generic;
using System.Text;

namespace Ordering.Data
{
    public class Address
    {
    }
}
```

Oops! Apparently I stubbed out the class, but forgot to add the actual properties. I need to put the rest of the properties into the file, which looks as follows:

```
using System;
using System.Collections.Generic;
using System.Text;

namespace Ordering.Data
{
    public class Address
    {
        #region Constructors

        public Address() { }

        public Address(string Address1, string Address2, string
          City, string State, string Zip)
            : this()
        {
```

```
        this.Address1 = Address1;
        this.Address2 = Address2;
        this.City = City;
        this.State = State;
        this.Zip = Zip;
    }

    #endregion

    #region Properties

    private int _id;
    public virtual int Id
    {
        get { return _id; }
        set { _id = value; }
    }

    private string _address1;
    public virtual string Address1
    {
        get { return _address1; }
        set { _address1 = value; }
    }

    private string _address2;
    public virtual string Address2
    {
        get { return _address2; }
        set { _address2 = value; }
    }

    private string _city;
    public virtual string City
    {
        get { return _city; }
        set { _city = value; }
    }

    private string _state;
    public virtual string State
    {
        get { return _state; }
        set { _state = value; }
```

```
        }

        private string _zip;
        public virtual string Zip
        {
            get { return _zip; }
            set { _zip = value; }
        }

        private Contact _contact;
        public virtual Contact Contact
        {
            get { return _contact; }
            set { _contact = value; }
        }

        #endregion
    }
}
```

15. By continuing to work my way through the errors that are presented in the
configuration and starting the project in Debug mode, I can handle each
exception until there are no more errors.

What just happened?

We have successfully created a project to test out our database connectivity, and an NHibernate
Configuration object which will allow us to create sessions, session factories, and a whole
litany of NHibernate goodness!

What is a session factory?

The NHibernate framework uses the abstract factory pattern (see http://en.wikipedia.
org/wiki/Abstract_factory_pattern) for creating sessions, and this factory is created
from a Configuration object.

The following line of code builds a Session Factory object from our configuration (cfg)
object that we'll use to create sessions:

```
ISessionFactory sessionFactory = cfg.BuildSessionFactory();
```

From now on, when we want to create a session, we just ask the `session factory` to open a session for us as follows:

```
ISession session = sessionFactory.OpenSession();
```

In addition to opening the session, we want to wrap our statements in a "transaction" to decrease database overhead. I know what you are thinking, wouldn't creating a transaction for every statement actually INCREASE database overhead? In reality, the database already uses implicit transactions for every call we make, so by explicitly telling it to create a single transaction for all of our operations, we are actually reducing the number of calls it makes. To create a transaction for our session, all we need to do is tell the session to begin a transaction for us:

```
ITransaction tx = session.BeginTransaction();
```

Creating your first session

Sessions in NHibernate aren't really too tricky, but they are INCREDIBLY powerful. With an NHibernate session, I can perform all of the CRUD (Create, Retrieve, Update, and Delete) operations with ease. Consider the following example:

```
ISession session = sessionFactory.OpenSession();
ITransaction tx = session.BeginTransaction();
Contact contact = new Contact("Joe", "Jones", "jj@nhibernate.com");
session.Save(contact);
tx.Commit();
```

With five short lines of code, we created a new contact and stored it into the database. The first two lines creates a `session` from the session factory and start a `transaction`, the third line creates the `contact` object from the `Contact` class that we created, and the last two lines commit it to the database. What if we wanted to add an address before we saved it? We would have to include another three lines of code as follows:

```
ISession session = sessionFactory.OpenSession();
ITransaction tx = session.BeginTransaction();
Contact contact = new Contact("Joe", "Jones", "jj@nhibernate.com");
Address address = new Address("123 USA St", null,
    "MainTown", "IL", "80305");
contact.Addresses = new List<Address>();
contact.Addresses.Add(address);
session.SaveOrUpdate(contact);
tx.Commit();
```

All we need to do is create the `Address` object, attach it to the `contact` object, and when we save the contact, the address also gets saved—automagically!

Instead of having to instantiate the `List<X>` on every object every time you use it, put some code in the getter of your property to handle it. The code for the `Addresses` property is as follows:

```
private IList<Address> _addresses;
public virtual IList<Address> Addresses
{
    get
    {
        if (_addresses == null)
            _addresses = new List<Address>();
        return _addresses;
    }
    set
    {
        _addresses = value;
    }
}
```

Why in the getter, you may ask? Simple, when you call `contact. Addresses.Add()`, it calls the getter of the `contact.Addresses` to retrieve the collection before it calls `Add()` on it. Our code says "if it's null, create a new list, then return it".

Did you notice that we used the `.SaveOrUpdate()` construct this time? When we create a new object, we can call `.Save()` to commit it to the database, and after we update it, we can call `.Update()`. However, if we don't want to be bothered whether it's new or not, we can just call `.SaveOrUpdate()` and let NHibernate determine if it is new and how to handle it appropriately.

Why do we call .Commit()?

I'm sure you are wondering why we keep calling `.Commit()` after we call `.Save()`. Basically, `.Commit()` closes our `transaction` and synchronizes the cached objects with the database.

We'll talk more about caching later, but in its simplest configuration, NHibernate uses a first level cache (or the session cache) to store objects. When you first query an object from the database, it is placed into this cache.

If you haven't told NHibernate to update or delete an object from the database, and it has already been cached, then it will pull this object from the cache rather than round-tripping to the database, improving performance.

By calling `.Commit()`, we let NHibernate know that we have updated the record(s) in the transaction and that it should persist them to the database.

NHibernate session versus database session?

An NHibernate session encapsulates and abstracts a database session. When we use NHibernate, we don't have to be concerned with many of the operations of the database to include SQL statements and even session manipulation. We let the session factory take care of all that database headache, and we just sit back and smile.

Time for action – creating a session and doing some CRUD

Now it's time to get to the real meat! We have spent the last four chapters "getting ready", and now we will actually create some data. Just like before, if you run into trouble (doesn't work like the walkthrough), see the troubleshooting section at the end of this *Time for action*.

1. Open the `Program.cs` or `Module1.vb` from the last *Time for action*, and scroll to the line that says `cfg.AddAssembly(typeof(Address).Assembly)`. On a new line, add the following code:

    ```
    ISessionFactory sessionFactory = cfg.BuildSessionFactory();
    ```

    In VB.NET, use this code:

    ```
    Dim sessionFactory As ISessionFactory = cfg.BuildSessionFactory()
    ```

2. Press *F5* or **Debug | Start Debugging** and test your project. If everything goes well, once again a command prompt window will pop up and then go away. If you happen to get an **InvalidProxyTypeException**, as shown in the following screenshot, it usually has to do with a property not being marked as "virtual" or "Overridable".

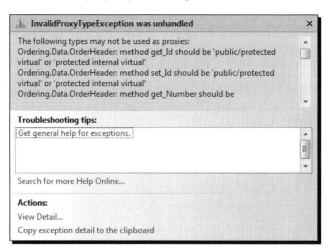

3. If this is your issue, then change your property to include the `virtual` or `Overridable` keyword as follows:

```
private int _id;
public virtual int Id
{
    get { return _id; }
    set { _id = value; }
}
```

Or in VB.NET:

```
Private _id As Integer
    Public Overridable Property Id() As Integer
        Get
            Return _id
        End Get
        Set(ByVal value As Integer)
            _id = value
        End Set
End Property
```

4. Once your project is able to create a session factory without throwing any errors, we are ready to go! Add the following code to your project and we can create a `contact` object and commit it to the database with only four lines of code:

```
ISession session = sessionFactory.OpenSession();
ITransaction tx = session.BeginTransaction();
Contact contact = new Contact("George", "Washington",
                              "gw@usa.gov");
session.Save(contact);
tx.Commit();
```

Or in VB.NET, it will be as follows:

```
Dim session As ISession = sessionFactory.OpenSession()
Dim tx as ITransaction = session.BeginTransaction()
Dim contact As New Contact("George", "Washington", "gw@usa.gov")
session.Save(contact)
tx.Commit()
```

5. Did it work? We have two ways of finding out, namely, using NHibernate or using SQL Server. Let's try SQL Server first. Open SSMS, and click on the **Ordering** database, then on **New Query** in the toolbar.

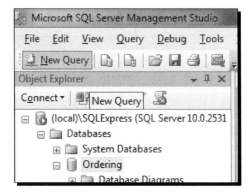

6. In the resulting query window, type the following query and either hit *F5* or click on the **Execute** button.

```
select * from Contact
```

7. The previous query should return one (or more, depending on how many times you ran the project) row(s). The returned rows should look as shown in the following screenshot:

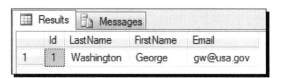

8. If we wanted to execute the same query from NHibernate, then we can add this code. Once we have the `IList` of `contact` objects, we can look at the `.Count` property of the `contacts` object to see how many items we retrieved. This can be done as follows:

```
ICriteria crit = session.CreateCriteria(typeof(Contact));
IList<Contact> contacts = crit.List<Contact>();
int contactCount = contacts.Count;
```

Once again, in VB.NET:

```
Dim crit As ICriteria = session.CreateCriteria(GetType(Contact))
Dim contacts As IList(Of Contact) = crit.List(Of Contact)()
Dim contactCount as Integer = contactCount.Count
```

Don't get too wrapped up in the `ICriteria` object right now, we will take an extensive look at it in *Chapter 8, Writing Queries*. It should suffice to say that it is used to query and filter data.

9. If we wanted to remove the objects we created, we can just iterate through them and call `Delete()`, while passing in each object. Add the following code into your project, and let's remove our contacts:

```
foreach (Contact ctc in contacts)
{
    session.Delete(ctc);
}
tx.Commit();
```

In VB.NET, it would look more like this:

```
For Each ctc As Contact In contacts
    session.Delete(ctc)
Next
tx.Commit()
```

10. Execute the code by pressing *F5*.

11. Go back to SSMS, and execute your `select` query again. As we deleted all of the contacts, the query should return zero rows.

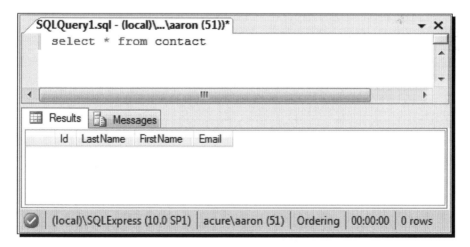

12. Now, let's create a slightly more complex object and save it to the database. Let's create an `OrderHeader` with an associated `Contact` that has an address and associate that `Address` and the `Contact` to the `OrderHeader`:

```
Contact ordCntct = new Contact("Martha", "Washington",
    "mw@usa.gov");
Address ordAddr = new Address("1600 Pennsylvania Ave NW", null,
    "Washington", "DC", "20500");
ordAddr.Contact = ordCntct;
ordCntct.Addresses = new List<Address>();
ordCntct.Addresses.Add(ordAddr);
OrderHeader header = new OrderHeader();
header.Number = "0000001";
header.OrderDate = DateTime.Now;
header.BillToContact = ordCntct;
header.BillToAddress = ordAddr;
header.ShipToContact = ordCntct;
header.ShipToAddress = ordAddr;
OrderHeader header = new OrderHeader("00001", DateTime.Now, -1,
    -1, ordCntct, ordCntct, ordAddr, ordAddr);
session.SaveOrUpdate(header);
tx.Commit();
```

Again, in VB.NET:

```
Contact ordCntct = new Contact("Martha", "Washington", _
    "mw@usa.gov");
Address ordAddr = new Address("1600 Pennsylvania Ave NW", null, _
    "Washington", "DC", "20500");
ordAddr.Contact = ordCntct;
ordCntct.Addresses = new List<Address>();
ordCntct.Addresses.Add(ordAddr);
OrderHeader header = new OrderHeader();
header.Number = "0000001";
header.OrderDate = DateTime.Now;
header.BillToContact = ordCntct;
header.BillToAddress = ordAddr;
header.ShipToContact = ordCntct;
header.ShipToAddress = ordAddr;
OrderHeader header = new OrderHeader("00001", DateTime.Now, -1, _
    -1, ordCntct, ordCntct, ordAddr, ordAddr);
session.SaveOrUpdate(header);
tx.Commit();
```

13. Now let's update our `OrderHeader` object and set the item quantity to ten items and update it.

```
header.ItemQty = 10;
session.Update(header);
tx.Commit();
```

It's nearly identical in VB.NET:

```
header.ItemQty = 10
session.Update(header)
tx.Commit()
```

14. As we're at it, let's change the order number to "chi3131":

```
header.Number = "chi3131";
session.SaveOrUpdate(header);
tx.Commit();
```

And the VB.NET is the same without the semi-colons:

```
header.Number = "chi3131"
session.SaveOrUpdate(header)
tx.Commit()
```

Pop quiz – creating and updating records

1. What object do we use to create new sessions?

   a. Configuration object

   b. E-mail object

   c. Session Factory object

   d. None of the above

2. Which command would save a record to the database?

   a. `session.Save()`

   b. `session.Update()`

   c. `session.SaveOrUpdate()`

   d. All of the above

3. How do we remove a record from the database?

   a. `session.Clear()`

   b. `session.Remove()`

   c. `session.Delete()`

   d. `tx.Commit()`

Have a go hero – creating a full order

Now that we know how to create objects and child objects of those objects and so on, let's take it one step further. Create a new `OrderHeader` object with a billing and shipping `Contact` with two separate `Addresses`, namely, one for shipping and one for billing. Create a few `OrderItem` objects and associate them with the `OrderHeader`. Save all of these objects to the database, then create an `ICriteria` and query it back and take a look at the objects that are returned.

Sessions in ASP.NET

Because of the stateless nature of ASP.NET, traditional session management doesn't work so well. If we try to create a single session and use it across several pages or requests, then this statelessness makes it more difficult for us to maintain this than it would in say a Winforms application.

There are a few strategies that we can use to overcome this, including implementing a Singleton pattern, storing the session in the user's Context, or using another framework such as NHibernate.Burrow.

The Singleton is probably the easiest to implement. We simply create a sealed class (meaning all of the member methods and variables are declared static) and create a property called `Instance`. Then, we create a non-static constructor that has the implementation details we want such as the `SessionFactory` property.

In C#, this `SessionProvider` class would look as follows:

```
public sealed class SessionProvider
{
  static readonly SessionProvider instance = new SessionProvider();
  public static SessionProvider Instance
  {
    get
    {
      return instance;
    }
  }

  public ISessionFactory SessionFactory { get; set; }

  public SessionProvider()
  {
    Configuration cfg = new Configuration();
    cfg.Properties.Add(NHibernate.Cfg.Environment.
      ConnectionProvider, typeof(NHibernate.Connection
```

```
      .DriverConnectionProvider).AssemblyQualifiedName);
    cfg.Properties.Add(NHibernate.Cfg.Environment.Dialect,
      typeof(NHibernate.Dialect.MsSql2008Dialect)
      .AssemblyQualifiedName);
    cfg.Properties.Add(NHibernate.Cfg.Environment.
      ConnectionDriver, typeof(NHibernate.Driver.SqlClientDriver)
      .AssemblyQualifiedName);
    cfg.Properties.Add(NHibernate.Cfg.Environment.ConnectionString,
      "Server= (local)\\SQLExpress;Database=ordering;
      Trusted_Connection=true;");
    cfg.Properties.Add(NHibernate.Cfg.Environment.
      ProxyFactoryFactoryClass, typeof(NHibernate.ByteCode.LinFu
      .ProxyFactoryFactory).AssemblyQualifiedName);
      cfg.AddAssembly(typeof(BasicWebApplication.Common
        .DataObjects.Address).Assembly);

    SessionFactory = cfg.BuildSessionFactory();
  }
}
```

The same factory in VB.NET is just as easy to include:

```
Public NotInheritable Class SessionProvider
  Shared ReadOnly m_instance As New SessionProvider()
  Public Shared ReadOnly Property Instance() As SessionProvider
    Get
      Return m_instance
    End Get
  End Property

Private _SessionFactory As ISessionFactory
  Public Property SessionFactory() As ISessionFactory
    Get
      Return _SessionFactory
    End Get
    Set(ByVal value As ISessionFactory)
      _SessionFactory = value
    End Set
  End Property

  Public Sub New()
    Dim cfg As New Configuration()
    cfg.Properties.Add(NHibernate.Cfg.Environment. _
      ConnectionProvider,GetType(NHibernate.Connection. _
       DriverConnectionProvider).AssemblyQualifiedName)
    cfg.Properties.Add(NHibernate.Cfg.Environment.Dialect, _
      GetType(NHibernate.Dialect.MsSql2008Dialect). _
      AssemblyQualifiedName)
```

```
    cfg.Properties.Add(NHibernate.Cfg.Environment.ConnectionDriver, _
        GetType(NHibernate.Driver.SqlClientDriver). _
        AssemblyQualifiedName)
    cfg.Properties.Add(NHibernate.Cfg.Environment.ConnectionString, _
        "Server=(local)\SQLExpress;Database=ordering; _
        Trusted_Connection=true;")
    cfg.Properties.Add(NHibernate.Cfg.Environment
        .ProxyFactoryFactoryClass, GetType(NHibernate.ByteCode.LinFu. _
        ProxyFactoryFactory).AssemblyQualifiedName)
    cfg.AddAssembly(GetType(BasicWebApplication.Common.DataObjects. _
        Address).Assembly)
    SessionFactory = cfg.BuildSessionFactory()
  End Sub
End Class
```

Now, to create a session, all we have to do is call as follows:

```
ISession session = SessionProvider.Instance.SessionFactory.
    OpenSession()
```

Another strategy is to store the session in the `Context.Items` using the `Application_BeginRequest` and `Application_EndRequest` methods in the `Global.asax` code or in an HTTPModule. I personally don't like these methods as much because it makes the ASP.NET application more difficult to troubleshoot, as you are adding an additional step in the lifecycle of the page.

One of the better frameworks for managing sessions (as well as other items like Units of Work, which we will talk about in *Chapter 12, Odds and Ends*) is NHibernate.Burrow. This framework is part of the NHibernate.Contrib project. You can find out more information about this framework and how to use it at `http://nhforge.org/wikis/burrow/home.aspx`.

Summary

We covered some great topics in this chapter that include:

- What is an NHibernate session?
- How does it differ from a regular database session?
- A little about retrieving and committing data
- Using sessions within ASP.NET

We also touched a little on configuration, caching, and session factories.

Now that we've learned about some basic data manipulation, we're ready to move on to logging, which is the topic of the next chapter.

6
I'm a Logger

According to the Apache project (http://www.apache.org), approximately 4 percent of all code written is for logging. This is a pretty significant number, especially if your application is of any real size. If we are going to write all of this code, we might as well use a framework that will make it easy for us to configure what gets logged, where we log it, and how much of it gets logged.

In this chapter, we'll talk about:

- Why do we need to log?
- Why log4net?
- Creating a logger
- Creating an appender
- Integrating NHibernate logging

Let's get started.

Why do we need to log?

Good question, glad you asked. We need to log a number of events, from simple instrumentation items, such as configuration times and application performance, to audit logging and application errors. All of these events tell us different things about our application or provide us with additional information, should we require it.

Why log4net?

There are three primary reasons for choosing log4net as our logging framework. First and foremost, it's an incredibly powerful logging framework with open extensibility. Second, it's open source so there is no charge associated with implementing or using it. Last, but not least, it's bundled with NHibernate because NHibernate uses it as its internal logging framework.

More information about log4net can be found at http://logging.apache.org/log4net.

If we are using log4net, we can simply set a few configuration options and access a number of interesting NHibernate internal log operations. One of the most helpful of these operations is the ability to view the SQL statements as they are generated. You can see a sample of this in the following screenshot:

As you can see, having access to this information is really useful. By knowing the SQL that NHibernate is executing, we can take this SQL statement and execute it directly in our SQL tool, such as SSMS, and see EXACTLY what is being returned to NHibernate. This helps us troubleshoot mapping issues, database design issues, and so on.

The SQL listed here is as follows:

```
SELECT shiptoorde0_.ShipToContact_Id as ShipToCo7_1_, shiptoorde0_.Id as
Id1_,

shiptoorde0_.Id as Id4_0_, shiptoorde0_.Number as Number4_0_,

shiptoorde0_.OrderDate as OrderDate4_0_, shiptoorde0_.ItemQty as
ItemQty4_0_,

shiptoorde0_.Total as Total4_0_, shiptoorde0_.BillToContact_Id as
BillToCo6_4_0_,

shiptoorde0_.ShipToContact_Id as ShipToCo7_4_0_

FROM OrderHeader shiptoorde0_

WHERE shiptoorde0_.ShipToContact_Id = 163842
```

If we execute this in SSMS, we can see the records that the database returned to NHibernate.

Getting started

log4net has three major objects that we need to be concerned with—the LogManager, loggers, and appenders. Imagine that log4net is a big bucket into which we throw all of the items we want to log on little scraps of paper. Instead of writing all of these pieces of paper by hand, we use an object called a logger. Loggers are used to classify and organize information as it is added to the bucket.

Once we have our information in the bucket, we need to get it out somehow, so we use an appender. Appenders take information from the bucket and "write" it out somewhere, depending on our configuration.

Multiple appenders can process the same log event and handle it in their own way. A couple of good examples of this are a Rolling File appender and an e-mail appender. If, for example, a high priority event is logged (such as a critical application error), then we may not only want to log it to a file, but also e-mail it to an administrator. We can configure appenders for each of these situations and many others that will be discussed later in the chapter.

To give you an idea of what kind of information log4net can provide about NHibernate, we add the following line of code as the first line of the `Main()` method of our Ordering. Console application. This gives us a lot of logging information automatically.

```
log4net.Config.BasicConfigurator.Configure();
```

With this simple code in place, the basic log4net configuration will be invoked, and as we are running a console application, it will be logged to the console. When you run the application, you will see a *lot* of NHibernate debug information scroll by. It should look something as follows:

Have a go hero – adding some logging

Try adding the following code to your `Main()` method of the console application, and then run it. Make sure you add a reference to the `log4net.dll` to your application (if it's not already there) and a `using log4net` statement at the top.

```
log4net.Config.BasicConfigurator.Configure();
```

Did your results look like those in the previous screenshot?

Configuration

Before we can actually do anything useful with log4net, we need to set it up. This basic configuration, much like NHibernate's own configuration, can be added in multiple places. log4net can be configured in code, as follows:

```
log4net.Appender.RollingFileAppender fileAppender = new
  log4net.Appender.RollingFileAppender();
fileAppender.Name = "GeneralLog";
fileAppender.File = "Logs/general.txt";
fileAppender.AppendToFile = true;
fileAppender.MaximumFileSize = "100KB";
fileAppender.RollingStyle = log4net.Appender.RollingFileAppender.
RollingMode.Size;
fileAppender.MaxSizeRollBackups = 5;
```

```
fileAppender.Layout = new log4net.Layout.PatternLayout("%d{HH:mm:
ss.fff} [%t] %-5p %c - %m%n");
log4net.Config.BasicConfigurator.Configure(fileAppender);
```

log4net is more traditionally configured from an `app.config` or `web.config` file, or as an XML file deployed with the application. This allows much quicker reconfiguration if additional logging is needed. For instance, if you are having an issue in production, you can simply flip the `level` flag on your file appender from `Error` to `Debug` and any additional logs that you have declared as `Debug` will now be added to that log file. This allows you to reconfigure logging while the application is still running, without having to deploy a debug build or attach a debugger to your application.

Application, web, and XML configuration files are all constructed the same way, using an XML type layout. The previous files' `appender` would look something as follows in the configuration file:

```
<appender name="GeneralLog" type="log4net.Appender.
RollingFileAppender">
  <file value="Logs/general.txt" />
  <appendToFile value="true" />
  <maximumFileSize value="100KB" />
  <rollingStyle value="Size" />
  <maxSizeRollBackups value="5" />
  <layout type="log4net.Layout.PatternLayout">
    <conversionPattern value="%d{HH:mm:ss.fff} [%t] %-5p %c - %m%n"/>
  </layout>
</appender>
```

The major parts of the appender has just declared that you need to be concerned with the `name` (`GeneralLog`) and the `type` (`log4net.Appender.RollingFileAppender`). These two items will be used to control what items get logged and what type of logging gets performed.

Time for action – adding some logging

In our Ordering.Console application of *Chapter 5, The Session Procession*, we were able to query data out of the database using a `ICriteria` object. We saw that NHibernate returned the data we asked for, but what if we wanted to know more? How do we see the SQL that was actually generated? Let's add some logging to our console application to show us the SQL that NHibernate generates.

1. Open the **References** folder of the **Ordering.Console** application. Is the log4net dll already referenced? If not, then right-click on **References**, click **Add Reference**, and browse to the `log4net.dll` that was included with the NHibernate release.

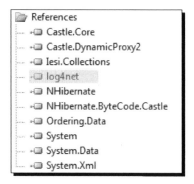

2. Right-click on the **Ordering.Console** application, and select **Add | New Item**. Select **Application Configuration File**, leave the name as `App.config`, and click on the **Add** button, as shown in the following screenshot:

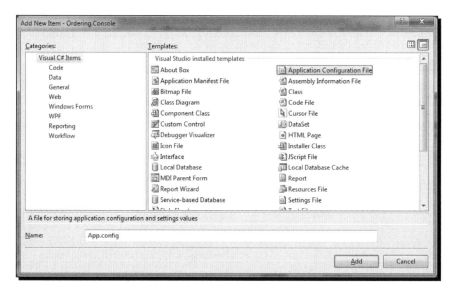

3. The first thing we need to add to our `App.config` file is a `<configSections>` tag inside the `<configuration>` section, with an additional closing `</configSections>` tag, as shown in the following code snippet:

```xml
<?xml version="1.0"?>
<configuration>
    <configSections>
    </configSections>
</configuration>
```

4. Inside our `<configSections>` block, we need to add a configuration section handler for log4net, so .NET will know how to interpret the log4net section we are going to create next. This simply says "when you get to a section named 'log4net', use the `log4net.Config.Log4netConfigurationSectionHandler` in the log4net assembly to process it".

```xml
<?xml version="1.0"?>
<configuration>
  <configSections>
    <section name="log4net"
      type="log4net.Config.Log4NetConfigurationSectionHandler,
      log4net"/>
  </configSections>
</configuration>
```

5. Next, under the closing `</configSections>` tag, before the closing `</configuration>` tag, we will add our log4net block, as shown in the following block of code:

```xml
<?xml version="1.0"?>
<configuration>
  <configSections>
    <section name="log4net"
      type="log4net.Config.Log4NetConfigurationSectionHandler,
      log4net"/>
  </configSections>
  <log4net>
  </log4net>
</configuration>
```

6. Inside our `<log4net>` block, we'll add a simple appender (in this case, it's the console appender). We'll talk more about the `<conversionPattern>` later, but basically, it controls the format of the messages. In this case, it displays the date (`%d{HH:mm:ss.fff}`), the ID of the thread the log came from in square brackets (`[%t]`), the priority of the log (`%p`), the class the message came from (`%c`), a dash (`-`), the content of the log message (`%m`), and a newline (`%n`).

```
<log4net>
  <appender name="Console" type="log4net.Appender.ConsoleAppender">
    <layout type="log4net.Layout.PatternLayout">
      <conversionPattern value="%d{HH:mm:ss.fff} [%t] %p %c -
        %m%n"/>
    </layout>
  </appender>
</log4net>
```

7. The last item we need to add to our application configuration is a `<root>` block. This is the "default" block for log4net, which will set up the basic configuration. Right after the `</appender>` tag, we'll add a `<root>` block and an `<appender-ref>` tag to tell log4net to activate the "Console" appender.

```
  </appender>
  <root>
    <appender-ref ref="Console"/>
  </root>
</log4net>
```

8. If you added the log4net configuration earlier in the *Have a go hero—adding some logging* section, then comment it out, as shown in the next line of code. If you didn't add it earlier, then don't worry, we don't need it.

```
//log4net.Config.BasicConfigurator.Configure();
```

    In VB.NET, comment the code as follows:

```
'log4net.Config.BasicConfigurator.Configure()
```

9. At the top of our `Main()` method, add the following line:

```
log4net.Config.XMLConfigurator.Configure();
```

    Or in VB.NET:

```
log4net.Config.XMLConfigurator.Configure()
```

10. Pressing *F5* or **Debug | Start Debugging** will execute the code, and you will see the following screenshot:

11. That's it! You've configured your first log4net XML configuration!

What just happened?

We just configured log4net using an XML configuration in the application configuration file. This is my personal favorite way to configure log4net because all of my configuration information is in the same place as my other application information.

We will learn more about filtering these messages and directing them to different appenders in the next few sections.

NHibernate log messages

Now that we have some basic logging configured, NHibernate spits out a lot of information. You will see various messages displayed such as "Using reflection optimizer" and "Mapping resource:". These messages let you know what NHibernate is doing, what stage of operation it is in, and what issues (if any) it encounters.

One of the first things you will see in these logs is the name of the assembly that we told NHibernate to read the mapping files from.

```
07:18:08.295 [10] INFO NHibernate.Cfg.Configuration - Mapping resource:
Ordering.Data.Mapping.Address.hbm.xml
```

As we included the `*.hbm.xml` files in the `Ordering.Data.Mapping` assembly, NHibernate is processing these files and logging as it processes each property of each file. NHibernate will list each of the properties in the mapping document, which class it belongs to, as well as the database field that is it being mapped to. An example of one of these mapping entries would look something like as follows:

```
07:32:49.299 [10] INFO NHibernate.Cfg.XmlHbmBinding.Binder - Mapping
class: Ordering.Data.Address -> Address
07:32:49.410 [10] DEBUG NHibernate.Cfg.XmlHbmBinding.Binder - Mapped
property: Id -> Id, type: Int32
07:32:49.474 [10] DEBUG NHibernate.Cfg.XmlHbmBinding.Binder - Mapped
property: Address1 -> Address1, type: String
07:32:49.479 [10] DEBUG NHibernate.Cfg.XmlHbmBinding.Binder - Mapped
property: Address2 -> Address2, type: String
...
6162 [9] DEBUG NHibernate.Cfg.XmlHbmBinding.Binder (null) - Mapped
property: Contact -> Contact_Id, type: Ordering.Data.Contact
```

This line says that the XML HBM Binding binder is being used to map the `Contact` property of type `Ordering.Data.Contact` to the `Contact_Id` field from the database. This can be useful to double check your mapping files and to make sure that they are doing what you think they should be.

While all this information is useful sometimes, most of the time it's information overload. Did you notice the various logging levels, INFO and DEBUG? While the INFO is fairly helpful to us, the DEBUG messages add a lot of useless chatter unless we are trying to debug a specific issue. How can we filter out these DEBUG messages you ask? Simple. We just need to tell log4net to only log messages at a priority *higher* than DEBUG, so we will add a minimum level to our root level log4net configuration.

```
<root>
    <level value="INFO"/>
    <appender-ref ref="Console"/>
</root>
```

By adding this *minimum* `level` tag, we filter out the `DEBUG` level entries, which helps make our log more readable:

Now each of the mapping classes displays on only three lines. As we usually need only a small subset of information to make sure NHibernate is doing what we think it should be doing, this minimal information is usually sufficient.

We can set the minimum level to any of the seven predefined levels: `ALL`, `DEBUG`, `INFO`, `WARN`, `ERROR`, `FATAL`, and `OFF`.

Appenders

There are a number of predefined appender types, from file and console appenders to telnet, database, and even e-mail. If there isn't a predefined appender that meets your needs, then you can write your own (as log4net is an extensible framework) and make it work any way that you like! I recently saw an appender that creates entries on the popular microblogging website Twitter.

Defining an appender is as simple as adding it to the configuration and telling log4net to write to it. If we wanted to log to a file, for example, we could use the Rolling File appender. I use the Rolling File appender all the time because you can configure it to rotate logs on a daily or size basis, along with numerous other options.

To define a Rolling File appender that will create a new log every day, we could use the following code:

```
<appender name="RollingLogFileAppender"
    type="log4net.Appender.RollingFileAppender">
  <file value="logfile" />
  <appendToFile value="true" />
  <rollingStyle value="Date" />
  <datePattern value="yyyyMMdd" />
  <staticFileName value="false" />
  <layout type="log4net.Layout.PatternLayout">
    <conversionPattern value="%date [%thread] %-5level %logger
        [%property{NDC}] - %message%newline" />
  </layout>
</appender>
```

This appender will create a log file with the name `logfile20200925` in the application directory. While this is useful, we can make it better. First, let's change the name of the `value` parameter of the `file` tag to include a path, and we'll also sneak a change into the `datePattern` tag to append `.log` to the end as follows:

```
<appender name="RollingLogFile"
    type="log4net.Appender.RollingFileAppender">
  <file value="logs\logfile" />
  <appendToFile value="true" />
  <rollingStyle value="Date" />
  <datePattern value="yyyy-MM-dd'.log'" />
  <staticFileName value="false" />
  <layout type="log4net.Layout.PatternLayout">
    <conversionPattern value="%date [%thread] %-5level %logger
        [%property{NDC}] - %message%newline" />
  </layout>
</appender>
```

By simply adding in a path and appending a literal string `'.log'` inside our double quotes at the end of the `datePattern`, we will now get a log file named `logs\logfile2020-09-25.log`, and this file will rotate every day, so tomorrow we will get a `logs\logfile2020-09-26.log`, and so on.

To activate this appender, all we have to do is go into our `<root>` block and add another `<appender-ref>` tag for our new appender as follows:

```
<root>
    <priority value="INFO"/>
    <appender-ref ref="Console"/>
    <appender-ref ref="RollingLogFile"/>
</root>
```

Now whenever our application is running, it will roll over into a new log everyday.

This setup is great and will log the same events to both the console and to our log file. What if I wanted a different logging level for the two? Say I still wanted INFO level log messages to display in the console, but wanted DEBUG level messages to go into the log file? Again, with log4net, it's pretty simple, if not blatantly obvious.

We need to remove the logging level from the root block, and instead, we can set a <threshold> on each of the appenders. Now our RollingLogFile appender will log DEBUG level and above messages. If we put a <threshold> block on the console and set it to INFO, we will have achieved our goal.

```
<appender name="RollingLogFile"
    type="log4net.Appender.RollingFileAppender">
  <threshold value="DEBUG" />
  <file value="logs\logfile" />
  <appendToFile value="true" />
  <rollingStyle value="Date" />
  <datePattern value="yyyy-MM-dd'.log'" />
  <staticFileName value="false" />
  <layout type="log4net.Layout.PatternLayout">
    <conversionPattern value="%date [%thread] %-5level %logger
        [%property{NDC}] - %message%newline" />
  </layout>
</appender>
```

If I only want DEBUG through WARN messages (DEBUG, INFO, WARN, and nothing else) to go to the console, I could do that with log4net too! All we have to do is add a filter to one of the appenders as follows:

```
<filter type="log4net.Filter.LevelRangeFilter">
    <param name="LevelMin" value="DEBUG" />
    <param name="LevelMax" value="WARN" />
</filter>
```

What if we only want information from a particular logger, such as NHibernate messages, to go into the rolling file log and everything else to the console? We need to create a new block in our configuration called a logger. We would divide our root block into two parts, a root and a logger block as follows:

```
<root>
  <priority value="INFO"/>
  <appender-ref ref="Console"/>
</root>
<logger name="NHibernate" additivity="false">
  <level value="DEBUG"/>
  <appender-ref ref="RollingLogFile"/>
</logger>
```

In this case, `NHibernate` is the name that NHibernate uses to log all of its internal messages. `additivity="false"` tells log4net to "use up" this message and not to pass it on to other appenders, so it will only show up in the appenders that are added in this block.

Why did I use level instead of priority in the logger, you ask? They are completely interchangeable. Either one will work in either block.

Pop quiz – creating and updating records

1. What do we use to make log4net logs visible to us?

    a. Appender

    b. Logger

    c. Session Factory

    d. None of the above

2. What XML tag acts as a log level or priority filter?

    a. `priority`

    b. `level`

    c. `filter`

    d. All of the above

3. How do we configure log4net?

    a. `App.config`/`Web.config`

    b. XML file

    c. Inline code

    d. All of the above

Creating a logger

If we want to log our own information using the log4net framework, we need to create a logger. Creating a logger of our own is actually quite simple.

Once log4net is configured, we simply call `LogManager.GetLogger(<type>)` and pass in the class type we are working with. For example, if we wanted to log the creation of a new `Address`, we would simply call `GetLogger()` to get a log object and then call one of the logging methods such as `Info()`.

```
private static ILog log = LogManager.GetLogger(typeof(Address));
...
log.InfoFormat("New Address Created: {0}", Address.Id);
```

This example uses the `InfoFormat()` method. Most of the logging levels
(`DEBUG`, `INFO`, `WARN`, `ERROR`, and `FATAL`) have these `Format()` methods, which take
multiple arguments (in the format of the `params` parameter list) that you can use to render
logs containing contextual information. These methods use the same constructs as the
`string.Format()` method.

 One thing to remember: While logging lots of information is great, logging
sensitive information such as SSN or credit card numbers can expose your
application to security concerns such as information leakage, so make sure
what you are logging is only what you need to get the job done.

In practice, I usually create an `ILog` variable `log` at the top of each class, so when I want to
use it, I am ready. An example of this in a simple class would be something as follows:

```
using log4net;
namespace Ordering.Console
{
  public class TestClass
  {
    private static ILog log = LogManager.GetLogger(typeof(TestClass));
    public int GetTestValue(string TestVal)
    {
      try
      {
        log.DebugFormat("Parsing value '{0}'.", TestVal);
        return int.Parse(TestVal);
      }
      catch (Exception ex)
      {
        log.Error("GetTestValue error occured", ex);
      }
      return -1;
    }
  }
}
```

You can see that we have a `public static ILog` variable named `log` and we are calling
`log.Error()` in the `catch` block. Now we can call logging methods (that is, `log.Debug`,
`log.Error`, and so on) in our code whenever a need arises.

Time for action – adding some custom logging

Now that we have all the key pieces of our application in place, let's add some logging information to our Ordering.Console application to give us some information about what's going on inside.

1. The first thing we need to do is add a `using` or `Imports` statement to the main class of our application.

    ```
    using log4net;
    ```

    And in VB.NET:

    ```
    Imports log4net;
    ```

2. Next, let's add a new logger to the class so that we can add logging messages. Inside the class or module, add the following code to get a local instance of the logger:

    ```
    private static ILog log = LogManager.GetLogger(typeof(Program));
    ```

    Once again in VB.NET:

    ```
    Private log As ILog = LogManager.GetLogger(GetType(Module1))
    ```

3. Now we're ready to log some data. Let's start out by adding some simple instrumentation timings. Let's find out how long it's taking us to configure NHibernate.

    Under the line `log4net.Config.XmlConfigurator.Configure()`, let's add a start time to base our timings on:

    ```
    Stopwatch sw = Stopwatch.StartNew();
    ```

    The VB.NET code is very similar:

    ```
    Dim sw As Stopwatch = Stopwatch.StartNew()
    ```

4. Next, on the line after the creation of the `ISessionFactory` in our code (about eight lines below the line we just added), we will add our first log message. Let's write out a DEBUG message that shows the amount of time it took to create our NHibernate configuration and build the Session Factory.

    ```
    log.DebugFormat("Configuration Time: {0}ms",
        sw.Elapsed.TotalMilliseconds);
    ```

    The VB.NET code is nearly identical:

    ```
    log.DebugFormat("Configuration Time: {0}ms",
        sw.Elapsed.TotalMilliseconds)
    ```

5. Now, if you run the console application, you should get a log entry that is similar to the one shown in the following screenshot. Notice that it took a little over five seconds for us to configure NHibernate and to create our Session Factory.

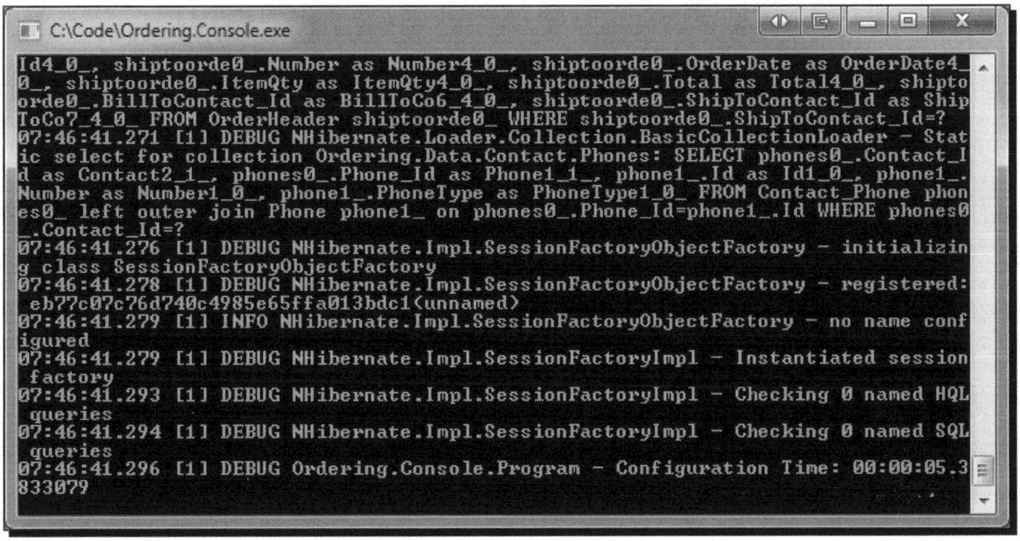

6. It seems like our timing logs might get lost in the ethos of all the other logs. Let's create a new logger specifically for `audit` logs and make our timing log to use our Audit logger.

Under the line where we created the static `ILog` log earlier, let's create a new `ILog`, but instead of passing it a type, we are going to pass it a string to create the log from as follows:

```
private static ILog audit = LogManager.GetLogger("Audit"));
```

Once again, in VB.NET:

```
Private audit As ILog = LogManager.GetLogger("Audit")
```

7. Back on the line where we added our logging before, we will change the line from `log.DebugFormat()` to `audit.DebugFormat()` as follows:

```
audit.DebugFormat("Configuration Time:
    {0}ms",sw.Elapsed.TotalMilliseconds);
```

8. Now, we can configure log4net to only log Audit messages to the console. In the App.config, create a new <logger> block. We will add two properties to the new block, the name "Audit" that we created earlier and the additivity "false". We also need to move the <appender-ref> tag for the Console appender from the <root> block to the <logger> block. This is done as follows:

```
<root>
  <priority value="ALL"/>
  <appender-ref ref="RollingLogFile"/>
</root>
<logger name="Audit" additivity="false">
  <appender-ref ref="Console"/>
</logger>
```

9. Run the application, and it should log a message, as shown in the following screenshot:

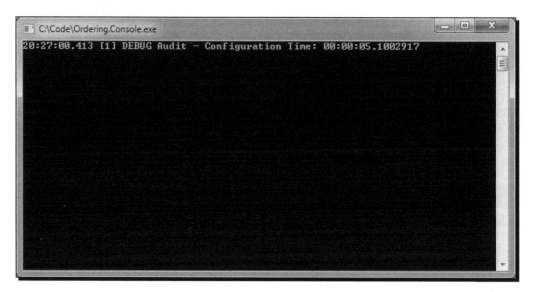

What just happened?

We have configured log4net to print not only NHibernate debug messages, but our own custom messages as well. By creating the Audit logger at a global level in our application, we can separate these messages or incorporate them into our own separate logs.

Have a go hero – adding some logging

Now that we have our custom logging configured, take a minute and log the NHibernate logger to a new rolling log file appender named "NHibernateFile". Make sure you add a new `<logger>` block for your file appender and tell it to only grab the NHibernate information.

Summary

We covered a lot of information in this chapter about logging and specifically log4net. By manipulating a few configuration items, we can modify not only what we log, but also how and where we log.

Specifically, we discussed:

- The reasons for logging
- Why we use log4net
- Creating loggers and appenders
- Integrating NHibernate logging into our own code

Now that we have our logging in place, we are ready to discuss the configuration of NHibernate in *Chapter 7, Configuration*.

7

Configuration

Configuration is simply a way to provide NHibernate with the information it requires to connect to the database, map our classes, and generally provide us with all of its benefits.

In this chapter, we'll discuss:

◆ Configuring in the `Web.Config`/`App.Config`

◆ Configuring in XML

◆ Configuring in code

◆ Logging SQL statements

So let's get on with it.

Looking back

If you remember, back in *Chapter 5, The Session Procession* when we talked about NHibernate sessions, we inserted some basic code to get us up and running that looked as follows:

```
Configuration cfg = new Configuration();

cfg.Properties.Add(NHibernate.Cfg.Environment.ConnectionProvider,
    typeof(NHibernate.Connection.DriverConnectionProvider).
    AssemblyQualifiedName);

cfg.Properties.Add(NHibernate.Cfg.Environment.Dialect,
```

```
            typeof(NHibernate.Dialect.MsSql2008Dialect).
            AssemblyQualifiedName);

    cfg.Properties.Add(NHibernate.Cfg.Environment.ConnectionDriver,
            typeof(NHibernate.Driver.SqlClientDriver).AssemblyQualifiedName);

    cfg.Properties.Add(NHibernate.Cfg.Environment.ConnectionString,
            "Server= (local)\\SQLExpress;Database=ordering;
            Trusted_Connection=true;");
    cfg.Properties.Add(NHibernate.Cfg.Environment.
            ProxyFactoryFactoryClass,typeof(NHibernate.ByteCode.LinFu.
            ProxyFactoryFactory).AssemblyQualifiedName);

    cfg.AddAssembly(typeof(Ordering.Data.Address).Assembly);
```

 Instead of using the `cfg.Properties.Add(..)` syntax, we can easily use `cfg.SetProperty(..)`. It takes the same syntax (`property name, value`), but it just looks a little cleaner.

This code creates a basic NHibernate configuration to SQL Server, but it has a few issues. The most glaring of these issues is our connection string, which is hardcoded into our application. If we need to change it, we have to recompile our code.

When we promote our application through the various levels of the **Software Development Lifecycle (SDLC)**, we usually have to go to different environments with different configuration requirements. It is usually easier to have this configuration information abstracted to another file. A separate version of this file can be maintained for each environment.

The basics of configuration

If you look back at our initial configuration in code, you will notice that there are five configuration options that we set. They are `ConnectionProvider`, `Dialect`, `ConnectionDriver`, `ConnectionString`, and `ProxyFactoryFactoryClass`. All of these elements have a property called `name` that we will use to set the value. We will set the same properties in the configuration file.

The property `ConnectionDriver` is usually not needed because setting the `dialect` will take care of driver settings using a sensible default.

These settings provide the basic information that NHibernate needs to get up and running. I like to call these the "Big 4 plus 1 (the mapping assembly)".

The `ConnectionProvider` property tells NHibernate what method it needs to use to build connections. This is usually set to "`NHibernate.Connection.DriverConnectionProvider`", but other providers can be used by providing the full classname of the provider (as shown) or adding the assembly name if it resides outside of NHibernate ("`MyCode.MyCustomProvider, MyCodeAssy`").

The `Dialect` property lets NHibernate know what database "language" it needs to speak. In our project, we are connecting to an MS SQL Server 2008 database, so we use the `NHibernate.Dialect.MsSql2008Dialect`. If we wanted to use MySQL instead, then we could substitute the `NHibernate.Dialect.MySQLDialect` dialect and we would be off to the races.

An interesting point to note here: To change the database provider with NHibernate is a one line configuration change. If you can create the same data structure, you don't need to change your code to port it to another database server. Moving from SQL Server to MySQL is as easy as recreating the tables in MySQL and changing the `dialect` and connection string!

The `ConnectionStringName` (and it's cousin `connection.connection_string`) give NHibernate the information about how to connect to the database. The `ConnectionString` property accepts a string that is the actual connection string, while the `ConnectionStringName` specifies a connection string in the `<connectionStrings>` section of the configuration that contains the connection string.

Using the `<connectionString>` section allows you to encrypt these values using the native Microsoft Encryption and Decryption provider. The easiest way to use these providers is to run the command line tool **aspnet_regiis.exe**.

```
c:\windows\Microsoft.NET\Framework\v2.0.50727\
aspnet_regiis -pef connectionStrings . -prov
DataProtectionConfigurationProvider
```

Decrypting is just as easy; use −pdf for decrypting instead of −pef for encrypting, and you don't need to add the provider name because it is already specified in the configuration file.

```
c:\windows\Microsoft.NET\Framework\v2.0.50727\aspnet_
regiis -pdf connectionStrings .
```

One note—the **aspnet_regiis.exe** tool looks for a file named `Web.config` instead of `App.config` in our project. We can trick it into working by simply renaming the `App.config` file to `Web.config`, running the command, and then changing the name back to `App.config`, and it works just fine.

Also noteworthy, this command is machine-specific unless you specify a new encryption key. You can override this key setting in your `App.config` or `Web.config` file, otherwise it uses the value in the `Machine.config`, which is re-encrypt. You will either need to override the setting or re-encrypt the file on each machine.

The `ProxyFactoryFactoryClass` is used to allow NHibernate to perform lazy loading. For example, if you have an instance of our `Ordering.OrderHeader` class and you access its `OrderItems` property, NHibernate will lazily load (retrieve from the database) all of the associated `Ordering.OrderItem` objects automatically, without you having to write another query.

Three basic proxy factories that come with NHibernate are as follows:

◆   `NHibernate.ByteCode.LinFu.ProxyFactoryFactory`

◆   `NHibernate.ByteCode.Castle.ProxyFactoryFactory`

◆   `NHibernate.ByteCode.Spring.ProxyFactoryFactory`

Most users will be perfectly happy with the LinFu proxy factory. Some NHibernate gurus think it has a slight speed improvements over the Castle DynamicProxy factory.

Castle DynamicProxy factory implementation was the standard NHibernate implementation for several years, and many NHibernate users still implement it. Castle will be useful to you if you decide to implement the Active Record Pattern using NHibernate. The Castle project has a full implementation of this pattern using NHibernate. You can find more information about it at `http://www.castleproject.org/activerecord/`.

The Spring ProxyFactory is used with the Spring **Inversion of Control (IoC)** framework, so unless you are using Spring, you won't need to use this one. More information is available at the Spring framework website— `http://www.springframework.net/`.

The final configuration property we need to add is the `mapping` property, with an element of `assembly` that contains the name of our mapping assembly.

A completed configuration will look as follows:

```
Program.cs

Ordering.Console.Program                                          ▼    Main(string[] args)

30    Configuration cfg = new Configuration();
31    cfg.Properties.Add(NHibernate.Cfg.Environment.ConnectionProvider,
32        typeof(NHibernate.Connection.DriverConnectionProvider).AssemblyQualifiedName);
33    cfg.Properties.Add(NHibernate.Cfg.Environment.Dialect,
34        typeof(NHibernate.Dialect.MsSql2008Dialect).AssemblyQualifiedName);
35    cfg.Properties.Add(NHibernate.Cfg.Environment.ConnectionDriver,
36        typeof(NHibernate.Driver.SqlClientDriver).AssemblyQualifiedName);
37    cfg.Properties.Add(NHibernate.Cfg.Environment.ConnectionString,
38        "Server= (local)\\SQLExpress;Database=ordering;Trusted_Connection=true;");
39    cfg.Properties.Add(NHibernate.Cfg.Environment.ProxyFactoryFactoryClass,
40        typeof(NHibernate.ByteCode.LinFu.ProxyFactoryFactory).AssemblyQualifiedName);
41    cfg.AddAssembly(typeof(Ordering.Data.Address).Assembly);
```

Pop quiz – basic configuration

1. Which of the following properties allows us to encrypt our sensitive configuration settings?

   a. `ConnectionStringName`

   b. `ConnectionString`

   c. `Dialect`

   d. None of the above

2. Which property can be added, but isn't usually necessary?

   a. `Dialect`

   b. `ProxyFactoryFactoryClass`

   c. `ConnectionDriver`

3. Which of the following is used for lazy loading?

   a. `ProxyFactoryFactoryClass`

   b. `ConnectionProvider`

   c. `Dialect`

   d. The world may never know

Taking a look at the SQL

Sometimes when we are troubleshooting issues, it's nice to look at the generated SQL statements. We can copy these out, execute them directly against the server, and find issues where we may have mistyped a value, flubbed a condition, or flipped a bit.

To make this configuration work, we just have to add the `ShowSql` configuration property to our configuration, and set it to `true`. In an inline configuration, the value would look as follows:

```
cfg.SetProperty( NHibernate.Cfg.Environment.ShowSql, "true");
```

This will add the SQL statements to our log4net loggers, which we can filter and direct, as necessary, from our configuration. If we add it to our existing `Ordering.Console` application, the resulting logs will look similar to the following screenshot:

One thing to note, the log4net logger `NHibernate.SQL` provides a much more complete SQL logging and is much preferred to using the `ShowSql` configuration property.

Have a go hero – using the connection string name

Having the connection string for our application hardcoded into our code is obviously a bad idea. If our password were to become compromised, we would have to recompile and deploy our application to change it.

Take a minute and convert the configuration in our `Ordering.Console` application to use the `ConnectionStringName` property, and create a `<connectionString>` with the same name in the `App.config` file.

Abstracting the configuration

One of the most common ways to configure NHibernate is to put the configuration into the `Web.config` or `App.config` file of the application. Other settings for your application are already stored here such as application settings in the `<appSettings>` block and database connection strings in the `<connectionStrings>` block.

By placing our configuration information in the `Web.config`, we can consolidate all of our configuration information together and take advantage of the available protections on that file such as cryptography and file separation, which we will talk about a little later.

In order to take advantage of mapping in the `Web.config` (or `App.config`) file, we need to add a configuration section handler declaration at the top of our configuration file, just like the one we added for log4net in the previous chapter. Inside the `<configSections>` element, we need to add a new `<section>` handler element with a `name` property of `hibernate-configuration` and a `type` property of `NHibernate.Cfg.ConfigurationSectionHandler, NHibernate`. It should look as follows:

```
<configSections>
  <section name="hibernate-configuration"
    type="NHibernate.Cfg.ConfigurationSectionHandler,
    NHibernate"/>
    ...
</configSections>
```

With the configuration handler in place for the `hibernate-configuration` section, we are ready to define that section. Inside our configuration file, we will add a section of type `hibernate-configuration` with a property of `xmlns` (XML namespace) that tells NHibernate what structure we will be using to create our configuration. The current version of this document is `nhibernate-configuration-2.2`. The code for this section would be written as follows:

```
<hibernate-configuration xmlns="urn:nhibernate-configuration-2.2">
</hibernate-configuration>
```

Inside this section, we need to add the `session-factory` configuration section. We will add the Big 4+1 properties to configure NHibernate, `connection.provider`, `dialect`, `connection.connection_string_name`, `proxyfactory.factory_class`, and `mapping`. A sample configuration for our application would be written as:

```
<hibernate-configuration xmlns="urn:nhibernate-configuration-2.2">
  <session-factory>
    <property name="connection.provider">
      NHibernate.Connection.DriverConnectionProvider
    </property>
    <property name="dialect">
      NHibernate.Dialect.MsSql2008Dialect
    </property>
    <property name="connection.connection_string_name">
      Ordering
    </property>
    <property name="proxyfactory.factory_class">
      NHibernate.ByteCode.LinFu.ProxyFactoryFactory,
      NHibernate.ByteCode.LinFu
    </property>
    <mapping assembly="Ordering.Data"/>
  </session-factory>
</hibernate-configuration>
```

To tell NHibernate to use our configuration, we just create a new `Configuration` object and call the `Configure()` method:

```
Configuration cfg = new Configuration();
cfg.Configure();
```

Our `Configuration` object is now configured, and our call to `cfg.BuildSessionFactory()` will function just like before.

Time for action – moving our configuration

Let's take a minute and convert the configuration from the `Ordering.Console` application to an `App.config` configuration.

1. Open the `Program.cs` or `Module1.vb` file, depending on which language you are using.

2. Comment out the existing `cfg.SetProperty` lines, using either the `//` or `'` depending on your language. Make sure you leave the statement where you "new it up" as we will use that again. When you are finished, your code should look as follows:

> You can use the comment button ▭ on the toolbar to comment out the selected code.

```
Configuration cfg = new Configuration();

//cfg.SetProperty("connection.provider", //"NHibernate.Connection.
DriverConnectionProvider");
//cfg.SetProperty("dialect", //"NHibernate.Dialect.
MsSql2008Dialect");
//cfg.SetProperty("connection.connection_string_name",
//"Ordering");
//cfg.SetProperty("proxyfactory.factory_class", //"NHibernate.
ByteCode.LinFu.ProxyFactoryFactory, //NHibernate.ByteCode.LinFu");
//cfg.AddAssembly(typeof(Address).Assembly);
```

Or in VB.NET:

```
Dim cfg As New Configuration()

'cfg.SetProperty("connection.provider", '"NHibernate.Connection.
DriverConnectionProvider")
'cfg.SetProperty("dialect", '"NHibernate.Dialect.
MsSql2008Dialect")
```

```
'cfg.SetProperty("connection.connection_string_name", "Ordering")
'cfg.SetProperty("proxyfactory.factory_class", '"NHibernate.
ByteCode.LinFu.ProxyFactoryFactory, 'NHibernate.ByteCode.LinFu")
'cfg.AddAssembly(GetType(Address).Assembly)
```

3. While we are in this class, let's add the new code that tells NHibernate to read from the configuration file. Under the code we just commented, add the following line of code:

```
cfg.Configure();
```

In VB.NET, it will look the same without the semicolon:

```
cfg.Configure()
```

4. Now we need to add our configuration properties to the App.config. If we were using a Web.config, the configuration would be exactly the same. Open the App.config, and find the <configSections> block. Add the ConfigurationSectionHandler section handler to this block. When you are done, the completed block should look as follows:

```
<configSections>
  <section name="hibernate-configuration"
    type="NHibernate.Cfg.ConfigurationSectionHandler,
    NHibernate"/>
  <section name="log4net"
    type="log4net.Config.Log4NetConfigurationSectionHandler,
    log4net"/>
</configSections>
```

5. Now NHibernate will be looking for the section named hibernate-configuration that we named above, so let's create that section by adding a <hibernate-configuration> block under the </configSections> tag.

```
<hibernate-configuration xmlns="urn:nhibernate-configuration-2.2">
</hibernate-configuration>
```

6. Inside the <hibernate-configuration> block, we need to add a <session-factory> section to define the configuration properties:

```
<session-factory>
</session-factory>
```

7. Next we need to define the "Big 4+1" properties, `connection.provider`, `dialect`, `connection.connection_string_name`, `proxyfactory.factory_class`, and the `mapping` assembly within the `<session-factory>` tags:

```
<property name="connection.provider">
   NHibernate.Connection.DriverConnectionProvider
</property>
<property name="dialect">
   NHibernate.Dialect.MsSql2008Dialect
</property>
<property name="connection.connection_string_name">
   Ordering
</property>
<property name="proxyfactory.factory_class">
   NHibernate.ByteCode.LinFu.ProxyFactoryFactory,
   NHibernate.ByteCode.LinFu
</property>
<mapping assembly="Ordering.Data"/>
```

8. When you are done, you should have a completed section that looks similar to the following screenshot:

```
<configSections>
  <section name="hibernate-configuration" type="NHibernate.Cfg.ConfigurationSectionHandler, NHibernate"/>
  <section name="log4net" type="log4net.Config.Log4NetConfigurationSectionHandler,log4net"/>
</configSections>
<hibernate-configuration xmlns="urn:nhibernate-configuration-2.2">
  <session-factory>
    <property name="connection.provider">NHibernate.Connection.DriverConnectionProvider</property>
    <property name="dialect">NHibernate.Dialect.MsSql2008Dialect</property>
    <property name="connection.connection_string_name">Ordering</property>
    <property name="proxyfactory.factory_class">NHibernate.ByteCode.LinFu.ProxyFactoryFactory,
    NHibernate.ByteCode.LinFu</property>
    <mapping assembly="Ordering.Data"/>
  </session-factory>
</hibernate-configuration>
```

9. Run the application by pressing *F5* or **Debug | Start Debugging**. The application should connect to the database and perform just like it did with the inline configuration.

What just happened?

Since we moved our configuration into a configuration file, we now have a lot more flexibility to integrate our code into the standard SDLC. We can use our build process to replace sections of the configuration with appropriate values for each environment (such as Development, Test, QA, Production), move the `<connectionStrings>` section to an external file, or other standard environment migration options.

XML configuration

Another common way to configure NHibernate is to put the configuration into an XML file. This is really simple, as it follows the exact same format as the `App.config`/`Web.config` files. All you have to do is create an XML file in your application and add the same settings that you would add to the `App.config` file.

```xml
<?xml version="1.0" encoding="utf-8" ?>
<hibernate-configuration xmlns="urn:nhibernate-configuration-2.2">
  <session-factory>
    <property name="connection.provider">
      NHibernate.Connection.DriverConnectionProvider
    </property>
    <property name="dialect">
      NHibernate.Dialect.MsSql2008Dialect
    </property>
    <property name="connection.connection_string_name">
      Ordering
    </property>
    <property name="proxyfactory.factory_class">
      NHibernate.ByteCode.LinFu.ProxyFactoryFactory,
      NHibernate.ByteCode.LinFu
    </property>
    <mapping assembly="Ordering.Data"/>
  </session-factory>
</hibernate-configuration>
```

To take advantage of this new configuration, we just call `Configure` with the name of the file:`cfg.Configure("NHibernate.xml");`

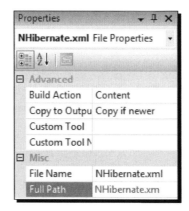

 One thing to remember, make sure you go into **Properties** for your XML file and set the **Copy to Output Directory** drop-down to **Copy if newer**.

Have a go hero – using an XML configuration file

Take the existing `App.config` file we created above, copy the `<hibernate-configuration>` section, paste it into a new XML file, and modify your `cfg.Configure()` statement to use the new XML file instead of the `App.config` file.

Summary

This chapter was all about configuration and the different ways to accomplish that task.

Specifically, we covered:

- How to configure NHibernate using the `Web.Config/App.Config` file
- Configuring NHibernate using an XML file
- Inline configuration of NHibernate in code
- Logging SQL statements using log4net

Now that our configuration is set, we're ready to create some real queries and retrieve exactly the data we want, which is the topic of the next chapter.

8
Writing Queries

Definitely one of the strongest reasons for switching to NHibernate has to be the way that you query data. By using simple constructions, we can build very complex queries with ease, without writing ANY SQL!

In this chapter, we'll spend a little time on:

- Data Access Objects (DAO)
- `ICriteria` queries
- The Fieldnames structure
- Projection

Let's get started!

Using Data Access Objects

When we originally created our Session object and wrote a couple of queries in *Chapter 5, The Session Procession*, we created all of our code inline. While this works for a simple sample, in a real application we don't want to embed this logic with our application logic, for a number of reasons.

Embedding our data access logic inside our application presents a few issues. Firstly, if we have our queries in the application, we can't reuse them in other applications without copying them. Second, by decoupling our presentation layer from our data layer, we can take advantage of technologies such as Silverlight and WPF more readily by using web services. Additionally, if we make any changes to our data layer, we would have to go back several places and change it in each place, instead of just fixing it in the data layer.

The basic Data Access Object

In order for our Data Access Objects to be effective for our use, they need to contain a few basic methods. In general, our DAOs will be responsible for all of the CRUD (Create, Retrieve, Update, and Delete) operations, so we will need to create methods to handle those operations.

We should add a local `ISession` variable called `Session` to allow easy access from our class. This gives us a single place to update in our class, should we decide to change the way we are handling sessions.

```
private ISession Session
{
  get { return SessionFactory.OpenSession(); }
}
```

The VB.NET code looks almost the same:

```
Private ReadOnly Property Session() As ISession
  Get
    Return SessionFactory.OpenSession()
  End Get
End Property
```

In order to make the interaction with our Data Access Object feel more natural to use, we need to do one more thing—add a Singleton object. Basically, we will create a property, called `Instance`, that will allow us to call the methods on our Data Access Object as if they were static methods.

So, instead of the following code:

```
ContactDataControl cdc = new ContactDataControl();
Contact contact = cdc.GetById(1);
```

we simply use:

```
Contact contact = ContactDataControl.Instance.GetById(1);
```

To make this happen, all we need to do is add the `Instance` property, which only has a getter.

```
private static ContactDataControl contactDataControl;
private static object lockContactDataControl = new object();
public static ContactDataControl Instance
{
  get
  {
```

```
lock (lockContactDataControl)
{
  if (contactDataControl == null)
  {
    contactDataControl = new ContactDataControl();
  }
}

return contactDataControl;
  }
}
```

In VB.NET, the code is as follows:

```
Private Shared contactDataControl As ContactDataControl
Private Shared lockContactDataControl As New Object()
Public Shared ReadOnly Property Instance() As ContactDataControl
  Get
    SyncLock lockContactDataControl
      If contactDataControl Is Nothing Then
        contactDataControl = New ContactDataControl()
      End If
    End SyncLock

    Return contactDataControl
  End Get
End Property
```

Now that we understand the basics of a Data Access Object, let's create one.

Time for action – creating our basic Data Access Object

Let's go back and remove our inline code from our previous applications and replace it with Data Access Objects.

1. Let's start off by cleaning up our `Program.cs` or `Module1.vb` class a little. We want to remove all of the code from the `Main()` method, except for the `log4net.Config.XmlConfigurator.Configure()` and the `Contact` and `Address` object creation. When you are done, your method should look as follows:

```
static void Main(string[] args)
{
  log4net.Config.XmlConfigurator.Configure();
  Contact contact = new Contact("Joe", "Jones",
    "joeyj@waywardone.com");
```

```
    Address address = new Address("2000 E. Captive Way", null,
        "Madville", "MA", "78701");
    address.Contact = contact;
    contact.Addresses = new List<Address>();
    contact.Addresses.Add(address);
}
```

The VB.NET method should look very similar:

```
Sub Main()
    log4net.Config.XmlConfigurator.Configure()
    Dim contact As New Contact("Joe", "Jones",
        "joeyj@waywardone.com")
    Dim address As New Address("2000 E. Captive Way", Nothing,
        "Madville", "MA", "78701")
    address.Contact = contact
    contact.Addresses = New List(Of Address)()
    contact.Addresses.Add(address)
End Sub
```

2. Now let's create our Data Access Object for the `Contact` object. Right-click on the **DataAccess** folder of the **Ordering.Data** project, click **Add | Class**, and name it **ContactDataControl**.

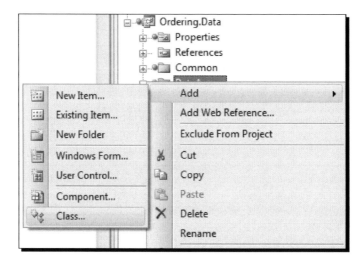

3. At the top of our class, we will need to define some imports. Add the following code to let .NET know about the `NHibernate` and `log4net` namespaces:

```
using NHibernate;
using NHibernate.Criterion;
using log4net;
```

And for our VB.NET brothers and sisters:

```
Imports NHibernate
Imports NHibernate.Criterion
Imports log4net
```

4. Now let's add an `ILog` in case we want to log anything from our methods along the way. Inside the `ContactDataControl` class, add the log4net logger code as follows:

```
private static ILog log = LogManager.GetLogger(typeof
    (ContactDataControl));
```

Once again, in VB.NET:

```
Private Shared log As ILog = LogManager.GetLogger
    (GetType(ContactDataControl))
```

5. Let's add in the `Instance` property so we can access this code without having to new it up:

```
private static ContactDataControl contactDataControl;
private static object lockContactDataControl = new object();
public static ContactDataControl Instance
{
  get
  {
    lock (lockContactDataControl)
    {
      if (contactDataControl == null)
      {
        contactDataControl = new ContactDataControl();
      }
    }

    return contactDataControl;
  }
}
```

In VB.NET, it looks like this:

```
Private Shared contactDataControl As ContactDataControl
Private Shared lockContactDataControl As New Object()
Public Shared ReadOnly Property Instance() As ContactDataControl
  Get
    SyncLock lockContactDataControl
      If contactDataControl Is Nothing Then
        contactDataControl = New ContactDataControl()
      End If
    End SyncLock

    Return contactDataControl
  End Get
End Property
```

6. Our Data Access Object wouldn't be very useful if it didn't have access to the NHibernate session, so let's add that next:

```
private ISession Session
{
  get
  {
    return SessionFactory.OpenSession()Session;
  }
}
```

The VB.NET property is really similar:

```
Private ReadOnly Property Session() As ISession
  Get
    Return SessionFactory.OpenSession()
  End Get
End Property
```

7. Now let's go back and repeat these steps to create Data Access Objects for the other four objects—Address, OrderHeader, OrderItem, and Phone.

What just happened?

We now have a base for a set of Data Access Objects that we can expand to cover all of the data storage and retrieval scenarios that we devise.

All we need to do now is add some logic to save, update, delete, and retrieve data, so let's get to it.

Data Access Object methods

We will need to create a `Save()` method to handle create and update operations, a `Delete()` method to handle deletions, and a few `GetX()` methods to retrieve data.

In order to implement the basic `Save()` and `Delete()` methods, we should do two things:

- Insert the logic for the method
- Wrap the method in a transaction

Why do we need to wrap it in a transaction? If something goes wrong and our action can't be completed, we can roll back the transaction and handle it in our code.

```
public int Save(Contact contact)
{
  ITransaction transaction = null;

  try
  {
    transaction = Session.BeginTransaction();
    Session.SaveOrUpdate(contact);

    transaction.Commit();
    return contact.Id;
  }
  catch (Exception ex)
  {
    log.Error(ex);
    if (transaction != null && transaction.IsActive)
      transaction.Rollback();
    throw;
  }
}
```

Adding our `Save()` method in VB.NET is just as trivial.

```
Public Function Save(ByVal contact As Contact) As System.Nullable
  (Of Integer)
  Dim retVal As System.Nullable(Of Integer) = Nothing
  Dim transaction As ITransaction = Nothing

  Try
    transaction = Session.BeginTransaction()
    Session.SaveOrUpdate(contact)
```

```
      If transaction IsNot Nothing AndAlso transaction.IsActive Then
        transaction.Commit()
      Else
        Session.Flush()
      End If

      retVal = contact.Id
    Catch ex As Exception
      log.[Error](ex)
      If transaction IsNot Nothing AndAlso transaction.IsActive Then
        transaction.Rollback()
      End If
      Throw
    End Try

    Return retVal
  End Function
```

As you can see, the `Save` method is pretty simple. We create a transaction, call `Session.SaveOrUpdate()` (letting NHibernate decide whether the object needs to be inserted or updated) and `Commit()` the transaction when we are done. If an error occurs, we can roll back the transaction and log the error.

The `Delete()` method is equally simple; all we do is change the save command to a delete command by calling `Session.Delete()` to remove the object from the database.

```
public void Delete(Contact contact)
{
  ITransaction transaction = null;

  try
  {
    transaction = Session.BeginTransaction();
    Session.Delete(contact);
    transaction.Commit();
  }
  catch (Exception ex)
  {
    log.Error(ex);
    if (transaction != null)
      transaction.Rollback();
    throw;
  }
}
```

The `Delete()` method in VB.NET is equally painless to implement.

```
Public Function Delete(ByVal contact As Contact) As Boolean
  Dim retVal As Boolean = False
  Dim transaction As ITransaction = Nothing

  Try
    transaction = Session.BeginTransaction()

    Session.Delete(contact)

    If transaction IsNot Nothing Then
      transaction.Commit()
    Else
      Session.Flush()
    End If

    retVal = True
  Catch ex As Exception
    log.[Error](ex)
    If transaction IsNot Nothing Then
      transaction.Rollback()
    End If
    Throw
  End Try

  Return retVal
End Function
```

Another method that is handy to have on our Data Access Object is a `Refresh()` method. This method will call the `Session.Refresh()` method on the object, forcing NHibernate to retrieve the latest object from the database directly instead of a potentially cached copy. This is useful if we have an outside process, service, or user that may be interacting with the database behind the scenes. This method can be simply implemented as follows:

```
public void Refresh(Contact contact)
{
  Session.Refresh(contact);
}
```

In VB.NET, the only real difference is the syntax of the language.

```
Public Sub Refresh(ByVal contact As Contact)
  Session.Refresh(contact)
End Sub
```

If we implement these basic methods on a new Data Access Object (one DAO for each of our data objects (POCOs)), we can quickly have a very functional Data Access library.

Time for action – adding some CRUD methods

Let's go back to our Data Access Object stubs we created earlier, and add some functionality to them.

1. We will start by defining a `Save` method that takes a `Contact` object as a parameter:

```
public int Save(Contact contact)
{
  ITransaction transaction = null;

  try
  {
    transaction = Session.BeginTransaction();
    Session.SaveOrUpdate(contact);

    transaction.Commit();

    return contact.Id;
  }
  catch (Exception ex)
  {
    log.Error(ex);
    if (transaction != null && transaction.IsActive)
      transaction.Rollback();
    throw;
  }

}
```

Our VB.NET code is also simple to implement:

```
Public Function Save(ByVal contact As Contact) As Integer
  Dim transaction As ITransaction = Nothing

  Try
    transaction = Session.BeginTransaction()
    Session.SaveOrUpdate(contact)

    transaction.Commit()
```

```
      return contact.Id
    Catch ex As Exception
      log.[Error](ex)
      If transaction IsNot Nothing AndAlso transaction.IsActive
Then
        transaction.Rollback()
      End If
      Throw
  End Try
End Function
```

The code for the `delete` method is as follows:

```
public void Delete(Contact contact)
{
  ITransaction transaction = null;

  try
  {
    transaction = Session.BeginTransaction();

    Session.Delete(contact);

    transaction.Commit();
  }
  catch (Exception ex)
  {
    log.Error(ex);
    if (transaction != null)
      transaction.Rollback();
    throw;
  }
}
```

The `Delete()` method in VB.NET is equally painless to implement.

```
Public Function Delete(ByVal contact As Contact)
  Dim transaction As ITransaction = Nothing

  Try
    transaction = Session.BeginTransaction()

    Session.Delete(contact)

    transaction.Commit()
  Catch ex As Exception
```

```
      log.[Error](ex)
      If transaction IsNot Nothing Then
        transaction.Rollback()
      End If
      Throw
  End Try
End Function
```

2. Let's go ahead and add a `Refresh` method to our Data Access Object in case we want to use it later. This is done as follows:

```
public void Refresh(Contact contact)
{
   Session.Refresh(contact);
}
```

The VB.NET code is as follows:

```
Public Sub Refresh(ByVal contact As Contact)
   Session.Refresh(contact)
End Sub
```

3. Now let's repeat steps 1 through 3 to add these methods to the Data Access Objects for the other four data objects: `Address`, `OrderHeader`, `OrderItem`, and `Phone`.

4. Let's go back to our `Program.cs` or `Module1.vb` and take advantage of the code we just added. First, we need to make sure our application knows about our data layer. Make sure you have the appropriate `using` or `Imports` statements at the top of your `Program.cs` or `Module1.vb` file as follows:

```
using Ordering.Data;
using Ordering.Data.DataAccess;
```

And in VB.NET, it is as follows:

```
Imports Ordering.Data
Imports Ordering.Data.DataAccess
```

5. At the bottom of the `Main()` method, let's add the code to save our `Contact` and `Address` objects.

Since the `address` is a child object of the `contact`, we just need to save the `contact` and the `address` will be automatically saved. Add this line of code under the `contact.Addresses.Add(address)` line:

```
intcontactId = ContactDataControl.Instance.Save(contact);
```

It is just as easy in VB.NET:

```
Dim contactId as Integer = ContactDataControl.Instance.
Save(contact)
```

6. Set a breakpoint on this line by clicking on the line and hitting *F9* or by right-clicking on the line and selecting **Breakpoint | Insert Breakpoint**.

7. Press *F5* or click **Debug | Start Debugging**, and the application should stop and wait at this breakpoint.

8. Press *F10* or click **Debug | Step Over** to allow the debugger to move to the next line.

9. Hover over the `contactId` variable, and you will see that our variable now contains an ID assigned by NHibernate (in my case 72, your results will vary), as shown in the following screenshot:

```
contact.Addresses.Add(address);

int? contactId = ContactDataControl.Instance.Save(contact);
}                    contactId 72
```

What just happened?

Now that we have the `Save` and `Delete` methods, as well as a `Refresh` method, we have the C, U, and D parts of the CRUD model implemented. Now we can go on to the retrieval methods.

Coding some GetX() methods

We want to have `GetById()` and `GetAll()` methods at least, as these methods are used frequently.

The simplest get method that we will code is the `GetById()` method, which is not just cleverly named, but should also retrieve an object by its ID. This method is really simple to code, because NHibernate already knows how to go get an object using its unique identifier.

To retrieve a record by its ID, all we have to do is call `Session.Get<T>()` and pass it an ID.

 If you haven't seen the `<T>` syntax before (or the `(Of T)` syntax in VB.NET), it is the .NET syntax for `generics`. It simply means ANY TYPE, so `<T>` for our `Contact` object would be `<Contact>` or `(Of Contact)`.

An example of the `GetById()` method would look as follows:

```
public Contact GetById(int Id)
{
   return Session.Get<Contact>(Id);
}
```

The VB.NET code looks very similar, we just substitute the `(Of T)` syntax for the `<T>` syntax of C#:

```
Public Function GetById(ByVal Id As Integer) As Contact
   Return Session.Get(Of Contact)(Id)
End Function
```

This is probably the simplest query we will have to write, as we are just re-packaging what NHibernate already gives us.

The FieldNames structure

One of the most useful things we can do (especially if we are using some sort of code generation to keep it in sync!) is to generate a FieldNames structure. One of the complaints that I hear from other developers coming to NHibernate is that the queries aren't strongly typed, so if the database structure changes or if they have a typo in their code, they won't know at compile time that they have broken code.

Traditional NHibernate queries are generally written as follows:

```
criteria.Add(Restriction.Eq("FirstName", fName);
```

In this case, if we change the field name in the database from `FirstName` to `FName` (and we don't adjust our mapping file, and leave `FName` to map to `FirstName` in our class), our code will compile just fine. However, when we run it, we will get a runtime exception because the `FirstName` field doesn't exist on our object.

One simple way to overcome this issue is to use a FieldNames structure, which simply maps string names of the properties to a local structure where we can access them. Instead of the previous code, our new query would look as follows:

```
criteria.Add(Restriction.Eq(FieldNames.FirstName, fName);
```

Now, if we change the name of the field, the `FirstName` field would be removed from our FieldNames structure and `FName` would be there instead. The compiler would throw an error because FieldNames does not contain a property "FirstName", and we would be able to fix it right there.

In C#, we define this as a structure because it's lightweight and efficient:

```
#region FieldNames

public struct FieldNames
{
   public const string Id = "Id";
   public const string LastName = "LastName";
```

```
    public const string FirstName = "FirstName";
    public const string Email = "Email";
    public const string Addresses = "Addresses";
    public const string Phones = "Phones";
    public const string BillToOrderHeaders = "BillToOrderHeaders";
    public const string ShipToOrderHeaders = "ShipToOrderHeaders";
}
```

```
#endregion
```

In VB.NET, we have two options. We can kludge it together using a structure, but we have to define a private property for it to work properly, or we can create a class.

```
#Region "FieldNames"

Public Structure FieldNames
    Public Const Id As String = "Id"
    ...
    Public Const ShipToOrderHeaders As String = "ShipToOrderHeaders"
    Private structureHolder as Boolean
End Structure

#End Region
```

You can also declare this as a Module, and it will be functionally equivalent, if slightly more resource intensive:

```
#Region "FieldNames"

Public Module FieldNames
    Public Const Id As String = "Id"
    ...
    Public Const ShipToOrderHeaders As String = "ShipToOrderHeaders"
End Class

#End Region
```

Personally, even with the small kludge, I like the structure because it's more lightweight and just seems a little cleaner. Whichever way you decide to choose, the FieldNames structure will save us time and headaches when trying to troubleshoot our code later.

Time for action – expanding our capabilities

Let's go back to our Data Access Objects we created earlier and give them a little more substance.

1. We will start by opening up the `ContactDataControl.cs` or `ContactDataControl.vb` as appropriate, and adding a FieldNames structure. At the top of the file, under the class declaration, add the following code:

```
#region FieldNames

   public struct FieldNames
   {
     public const string Id = "Id";
     public const string LastName = "LastName";
     public const string FirstName = "FirstName";
     public const string Email = "Email";
     public const string Addresses = "Addresses";
     public const string Phones = "Phones";
     public const string BillToOrderHeaders = "BillToOrderHeaders";
     public const string ShipToOrderHeaders = "ShipToOrderHeaders";
   }

#endregion
```

The VB.NET structure will look as follows (don't forget the private variable):

```
#Region "FieldNames"

   Public Structure FieldNames
     Public Const Id As String = "Id"
     Public Const LastName As String = "LastName"
     Public Const FirstName As String = "FirstName"
     Public Const Email As String = "Email"
     Public Const Addresses As String = "Addresses"
     Public Const Phones As String = "Phones"
     Public Const BillToOrderHeaders As String =
       "BillToOrderHeaders"
     Public Const ShipToOrderHeaders As String =
       "ShipToOrderHeaders"
     Private structureHolder As Boolean
   End Structure

#End Region
```

2. Next we will add the code for our `GetById()` method so we can retrieve individual records. Add the following code to the class after the `Delete()` method we created earlier:

```
public Contact GetById(int Id)
{
   return Session.Get<Contact>(Id);
}
```

The VB.NET code looks very similar, we just substitute the `(Of T)` syntax for the `<T>` syntax of C#:

```
Public Function GetById(ByVal Id As Integer) As Contact
   Return Session.Get(Of Contact)(Id)
End Function
```

3. Let's go back to our `Program.cs` or `Module1.vb` file and test our new code. In the `Program.cs` file, after the line: `int? contactId = ContactDataControl.Instance.Save(contact);` add the following code:

```
Contact retContact = ContactDataControl.Instance.
GetById(contactId.Value);
```

In VB.NET, under the line that reads `Dim contactId As System.Nullable(Of Integer) = ContactDataControl.Instance.Save(contact)` add

```
Dim retContact As Contact = ContactDataControl.Instance.
GetById(contactId.Value)
```

4. Set a breakpoint on this line by clicking on the line and hitting *F9* or right-clicking on the line and selecting **Breakpoint | Insert Breakpoint**.

5. Press *F5* or click **Debug | Start Debugging** and the application should stop and wait at this breakpoint.

6. Press *F10* or click **Debug | Step Over** to allow the debugger to move to the next line.

7. Hover over the `retContact` variable, and you will see that our variable now contains the full Contact record:

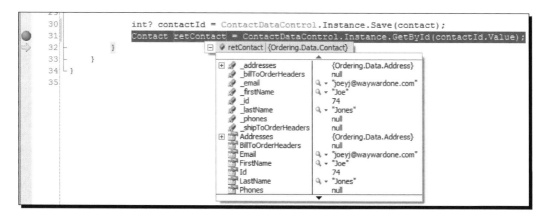

What just happened?

We created a `GetById()` method and a FieldNames structure, and we were able to use that `GetById()` method to retrieve a record that we inserted.

Now we are ready to move on to some SERIOUS querying.

The ICriteria object

In my opinion, the best way to write queries with NHibernate is to use a criteria object. The `ICriteria` object is created from a session, using the syntax `Session. CreateCriteria<T>()` or `Session.CreateCriteria(Of T)()`. By passing in a type, we basically tell NHibernate what type of objects we will be querying. For example, the following code:

```
ICriteria criteria = Session.CreateCriteria<Contact>();
```

would evaluate to a pseudo-SQL query of:

```
SELECT * FROM Contact;
```

Once we have an `ICriteria` object built, we can simply ask it to retrieve the requested records for us. If we want it to return a list of objects, in this case, a list of `Contact` objects, we simply call `criteria.List<T>()` or `criteria.List(Of T)()`.

```
IList<Contact> contacts = criteria.List<Contact>();
```

If we expect our query to return a single record and to return NULL otherwise, we can tell NHibernate to return a `UniqueResult<type>()`.

```
Contact contact = criteria.UniqueResult<Contact>();
```

These three pieces of code will be used OVER and OVER in our query methods, so it's a good thing they are easy to use!

Pop quiz – FieldNames and ICriteria

1. Why do we create a FieldNames structure?
    a. Looks cool
    b. To provide consistency in property name strings
    c. To change database field names
    d. We shouldn't

2. How do we get a collection of entities from our `ICriteria` object?
    a. `criteria.Query()`
    b. `criteria.IList<T>()`
    c. `criteria.List<T>()`
    d. `criteria.GetAll()`

3. How many records will `criteria.UniqueResult<T>()` return?
    a. Exactly one
    b. Zero
    c. Zero or one (or an Exception)
    d. Impossible to tell

Creating a GetAll() method

To make our Data Access Object more functional, we will need to create our `GetAll()` method that simply returns all records. We will also want to create `GetAll()` and `GetCountOfAll()` methods with some additional parameters that will let us take advantage of the paging functionality of the ASP.NET framework controls when we have larger result sets.

Using an `ICriteria` object, it's really simple to write a `GetAll()` method. All we have to do is new up an `ICriteria` object, and call `.List<T>()` on it. It will retrieve all of the objects of that type. The code for our `GetAll()` method would look like this:

```
public IList<Contact> GetAll()
{
  ICriteria criteria = Session.CreateCriteria<Contact>();
  return criteria.List<Contact>();
}
```

It is just as simple in VB.NET:

```
Public Function GetAll() As IList(Of Contact)
   Dim criteria As ICriteria = Session.CreateCriteria(Of Contact)()
   Return criteria.List(Of Contact)()
End Function
```

To create a `GetCountOfAll()` method, we are going to use something new, a `Projection`. Basically, a projection says "instead of retrieving the records, just grab the information I am asking for". This is usually an aggregate of some sort, such as a count of records, the sum of a field, and so on. The following image shows a list of the projections available in the `Projections` class.

Some of the more common projections we use are `Projections.RowCount()` and `Projections.Distinct()`. In order to get the record count for our `GetCountOfAll()` method, we just need to create an `ICriteria`, call `.SetProjection()` on the `ICriteria`, tell it we need a `RowCount()` projection, and ask for the result. The code looks as follows:

```
public int GetCountOfAll()
{
   ICriteria criteria = Session.CreateCriteria<Contact>();
   int result = (int)criteria.SetProjection(Projections.RowCount()).
                  UniqueResult();
   return result;
}
```

The VB.NET code is so similar, you probably don't even need to see it, but here it is:

```
Public Function GetCountAll() As Integer
   Dim criteria As ICriteria = Session.CreateCriteria(Of Contact)()
   Dim result As Integer =
      CInt(criteria.SetProjection(Projections.RowCount()).
      UniqueResult())
   Return result
End Function
```

Now we have some simple `GetAll()` and a `GetCountOfAll()` methods that will return every object in the database and the count of those objects.

Paging and Sorting GetAll() methods

The `GetAll()` methods mentioned earlier are very useful, but what if we only want a subset of those records? For example, what if we want the first 25 instances, then the next 25, and so on? This happens a lot in ASP.NET applications when we want to return paginated data 25 records at a time, instead of an entire list of 5,000 records.

In order to make this work, we simply need to tell the criteria what record to start returning from, and how many records to return. With one more variable, `SortExpression`, we can tell it to sort the records also, so that paging and sorting can be added to our data-bound controls such as the gridview.

To make this work, we need to pass in an integer for `firstResult` to return, a second integer for the `maxResults` to return, and a string for the `sortExpression`.

When ASP.NET passes the sort criteria, it is in the form "SORT_FIELD" or "SORT_FIELD<space>DESC". We need to split this field on the space, and if the second field exists and contains "DESC", then we need to sort descending; otherwise, we will sort ascending.

The code for this is easier to read than the explanation. It is as follows:

```csharp
public IList<Contact> GetAll(int firstResult, int maxResults,
    string sortExpression)
{
  ICriteria criteria = Session.CreateCriteria<Contact>();

  if (!String.IsNullOrEmpty(sortExpression))
  {
    string[] sort = sortExpression.Split(' ');
    bool ascending = true;
    if (sort.Length > 1 && sort[1].ToUpper() == "DESC")
    {
      ascending = false;
    }
    criteria.AddOrder(new NHibernate.Criterion.Order(sort[0],
      ascending));
  }

  if (firstResult != 0)
    criteria.SetFirstResult(firstResult);

  if (maxResults != 0)
    criteria.SetMaxResults(maxResults);

  return criteria.List<Contact>();
}
```

The VB.NET code is nearly identical:

```vbnet
Public Function GetAll(ByVal firstResult As Integer, ByVal maxResults
As Integer, ByVal sortExpression As String) As IList(Of Contact)
  Dim criteria As ICriteria = Session.CreateCriteria(Of Contact)()

  If Not String.IsNullOrEmpty(sortExpression) Then
    Dim sort As String() = sortExpression.Split(" "c)
    Dim ascending As Boolean = True
    If sort.Length > 1 AndAlso sort(1).ToUpper() = "DESC" Then
      ascending = False
    End If
    criteria.AddOrder(New NHibernate.Criterion.Order(sort(0),
      ascending))
  End If

  If firstResult <> 0 Then
    criteria.SetFirstResult(firstResult)
```

```
   End If

   If maxResults <> 0 Then
      criteria.SetMaxResults(maxResults)
   End If

   Return criteria.List(Of Contact)()
End Function
```

Now we have sorting and paging methods that we can duplicate in our other Data Access Objects.

Have a go hero – creating some paging and sorting methods

Take a few minutes and code up the `GetAll()`, `GetAll(int,int,string)`, and `GetCountOfAll()` in our Contact Data Access Object. When you are done, go back to the `Program.cs` or `Module1.vb` and use the `ContactDataControl.Instance.GetAll()` method to return an `IList<Contact>` (or `IList(Of contact)`).

Filtering ICriteria

Our `GetById()` and `GetAll()` methods are great, and they do just what we want, but what if we want more? What if we don't want all of the Contacts, but only those that have a first name of "Joe", or birthdays between the 1st of January and 31st of December in 1990? That's where we can use things such as `Restrictions` in NHibernate to "trim down" the collection of results.

One of the most common filtering actions is to restrict the result set to a particular value, or a something that contains a particular value. If we wanted to only get Contacts with the first name "Joe", we could create the following query:

```
ICriteria criteria = Session.CreateCriteria<Contact>();
criteria.Add(Restrictions.Eq(FieldNames.FirstName, "Joe"));
return criteria.List<Contact>();
```

If we wanted everyone who has a first name that starts with "Joe", we could change it to:

```
ICriteria criteria = Session.CreateCriteria<Contact>();
criteria.Add(Restrictions.Like(FieldNames.FirstName, "Joe%"));
return criteria.List<Contact>();
```

And if we had multiple criteria, such as a first name that starts with A and born between 1/1/1990 and 12/31/1990, we can just add that as follows:

```
ICriteria criteria = Session.CreateCriteria<Contact>();
criteria.Add(Restrictions.Like(FieldNames.FirstName, "A%"));
criteria.Add(Restrictions.Between(FieldNames.BirthDate, new
DateTime(1990,01,01), new DateTime(1990,12,31)));
return criteria.List<Contact>();
```

We can add as many additional restrictions as we need to accomplish the needs of our query. But, what if we wanted to find all of the contacts that live in the state of "MA"? This data isn't part of the `Contact` object, but it's related `Addresses` property. How do we add this filter, you ask? We simply create another `ICriteria` object, while using our original `ICriteria` object instead of the session. It will look something like this:

```
ICriteria criteria = Session.CreateCriteria<Contact>();
ICriteria addrCriteria =
   criteria.CreateCriteria(FieldNames.Addresses);
addrCriteria.Add(Restrictions.Eq(AddressDataControl.
   FieldNames.State, "MA"));
return criteria.List<Contact>();
```

If you don't want to use the new `ICriteria` again, then you can just string the command together as follows:

```
ICriteria criteria = Session.CreateCriteria<Contact>(); criteria.Creat
eCriteria(FieldNames.Addresses).Add(Restrictions.Eq
   (AddressDataControl.FieldNames.State, "MA"));
return criteria.List<Contact>();
```

There are a number of additional restrictions, such as "Greater Than" (`Restrictions.Gt`), "Greater Than or Equal To" (`Restrictions.Ge`), "In" (`Restrictions.In`), and "Not" (`Restrictions.Not`). These restrictions can be combined. For example, the code for "Where the First Name does NOT start with 'A'" is as follows:

```
ICriteria criteria = Session.CreateCriteria<Contact>();
criteria.Add(Restrictions.Not(Restrictions.Like
   (FieldNames.FirstName, "A%")));
return criteria.List<Contact>();
```

Did you notice the "%" sign above? If you are not familiar with SQL syntax, this is a wildcard character. When used with the function `Like`, we can restrict the data to find precisely what we need. For example, if I wanted to find all of the instances that started with "A", I could use `Like("A%")`. If I wanted to find all the instances that ENDED with "ing", I could say `Like("%ing")`. Similarly, if I wanted all the instances with an "X" in the middle, I could use `Like("%X%")`.

amazon.co.uk

CWF58

Thank you for shopping at Amazon.co.uk!

Invoice for
Your order of 13 July, 2010
Order ID 026-1883350-7999526
Invoice number DjD5J8rWR
Invoice date 13 July, 2010

Billing Address
simon bellis
24 The Heathers
Boughton
Newark, Nottinghamshire NG22 9HE
United Kingdom

Shipping Address
simon bellis
24 The Heathers
Boughton
Newark, Nottinghamshire NG22 9HE
United Kingdom

Qty.	Item	Our Price (excl. VAT)	VAT Rate	Total Price
1	**NHibernate 2: Beginner's Guide** Paperback. Cure, Aaron. 1847198902 (** P-1-E90D85 **)	£27.99	0%	£27.99
	Shipping charges	£2.75	0%	£2.75
	Subtotal (excl. VAT) 0%			£30.74
	Total VAT			£0.00
	Total			£30.74

Conversion rate - £1.00 : EUR 1,20

This shipment completes your order.

You can always check the status of your orders or change your account details from the "Your Account" link at the top of each page on our site.

Thinking of returning an item? PLEASE USE OUR ON-LINE RETURNS SUPPORT CENTRE.

Our Returns Support Centre (www.amazon.co.uk/returns-support) will guide you through our Returns Policy and provide you with a printable personalised return label. Please have your order number ready (you can find it next to your order summary, above). Our Returns Policy does not affect your statutory rights.

Amazon EU S.à r.l; 5, Rue Plaetis. L - 2338 Luxembourg
VAT number : GB727255821
Please note - this is not a returns address - for returns - please see above for details of our online returns centre

31/DjD5J8rWR/-1 of 1-//1MN/std-uk-dom/5660750/0714-17:30/0713-14:58 Pack Type : CWF58

Much more information and some great examples are included in the NHibernate documentation, but you should have enough information here to get started.

Time for action – replacing our inline code

As we have a working Data Access Object, we can now go in and create the custom methods we need for a particular function.

1. Open up the `ContactDataControl.cs` or `ContactDataControl.vb` again, and let's go down to the bottom of the class, just before the end.

2. Let's create a new function to return all of the Contacts that have addresses in a particular state, and we will pass that state with a `string` variable. Add the following method to your code:

```
public IList<Contact> GetByState(string State)
{
  ICriteria criteria = Session.CreateCriteria<Contact>();
  criteria.CreateCriteria(FieldNames.Addresses).Add
    (Restrictions.Eq(AddressDataControl.FieldNames.State, State));
  return criteria.List<Contact>();
}
```

If you are working in VB.NET, add the following code:

```
Public Function GetByState(ByVal State As String) As IList(Of
  Contact)
  Dim criteria As ICriteria = Session.CreateCriteria(Of Contact)()
  criteria.CreateCriteria(FieldNames.Addresses).Add
    (Restrictions.Eq(AddressDataControl.FieldNames.State, State))
  Return criteria.List(Of Contact)()
End Function
```

3. Let's go back to our `Program.cs` or `Module1.vb` file and test out our new code. In the `Program.cs` file, after the line where we retrieved our `Contact` object by ID, add the following code:

```
IList<Contact> stateContacts =
  ContactDataControl.Instance.GetByState("VT");
```

In VB.NET add the following code:

```
Dim stateContacts As IList(Of Contact) =
  ContactDataControl.Instance.GetByState("VT")
```

4. Set a breakpoint on this line by clicking on the line and hitting *F9* or right-clicking on the line and selecting **Breakpoint | Insert Breakpoint**.

5. Press *F5* or click **Debug | Start Debugging** and the application should stop and wait at this breakpoint.

6. Press *F10* or click **Debug | Step Over** to allow the debugger to move to the next line.

7. Hover over the `stateContacts` variable. Does it contain anything? Nope, it's NULL, because there are no Contacts that live in "Vermont".

8. Now let's change the "VT" in our code to "MA", and execute it again. Now we get some results, as we can see by hovering over the `stateContacts` variable again.

What just happened?

We are now able to write custom queries to retrieve collections of data from whatever portions of the system we want, and filter that data any which way.

Summary

We have covered a lot of information in this chapter: several ways to write queries, format them, and how to retrieve the data that we want.

Specifically, we covered:

♦ The need for and how to create basic Data Access (DA) objects

♦ Creating NHibernate Queries using ICriteria objects

♦ Using the Fieldnames structure to help eliminate coding issues

♦ How to use projection to retrieve record counts

Now that we are experts at writing NHibernate queries to retrieve data, we can move on to DataBinding, or tying our data to controls in ASP.NET and Windows Forms, which is the topic of the next chapter.

9
Binding Data

One of the most common tasks we are asked as programmers to perform is to display data on a web page or a windows form. Data binding on the Web or in a windows form isn't all that difficult. In most cases, it's a simple matter of retrieving the data you want to display, telling the control how to display it, and letting the magic happen.

In this chapter, we are going to talk about:

- ◆ Data Binding techniques
    - ❏ `<asp:ListView>`
    - ❏ `<asp:ObjectDataSource>`

- ◆ Direct Data Binding
    - ❏ `<asp:GridView>`
    - ❏ `<asp:Repeater/asp:DataList>`
    - ❏ `<asp:DropDownList/asp:CheckBoxList>`
    - ❏ `<asp:FormView>`

Let's get started!

Why should we use data binding?

Data binding is pretty simple and one of my personal favorite features of ASP.NET. By adding a few simple controls to my page and setting a few properties, my HTML page can become a dynamic, "living" page. I can add data to the database and have it displayed on my page, formatted in any way I want.

Imagine creating a website for your favorite club, and like most clubs, they need a calendar for upcoming events. If you define this in a web page and need to go in every time someone wants to add an event and change the page, how long do you think you would want to be the webmaster?

Wouldn't it be easier on the webmaster if we just create a web page, which is bound to a database table, and allow members to add their own events to the database?

Time for action – adding an ASP.NET project

Before we can create any ASP.NET controls to bind data to, we need to have an ASP.NET web application to hold them. Let's create a web application project to use in the rest of our examples.

1. Right-click on the **Ordering** solution, and click **Add | New Project**.

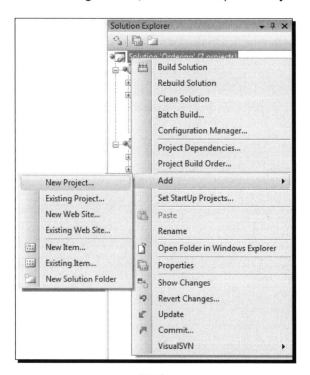

2. Select **ASP.NET Web Application**, and name it **Ordering.Web**, as shown in the following screenshot:

The primary advantage of an ASP. NET Web Application over a traditional website project is that the code is precompiled, so you don't have to publish your source code to your website. Additionally, IIS is not needed to run the website project from inside Visual Studio for debugging, so you don't need to go through setting up a virtual directory and so on, thus making the initial setup simpler.

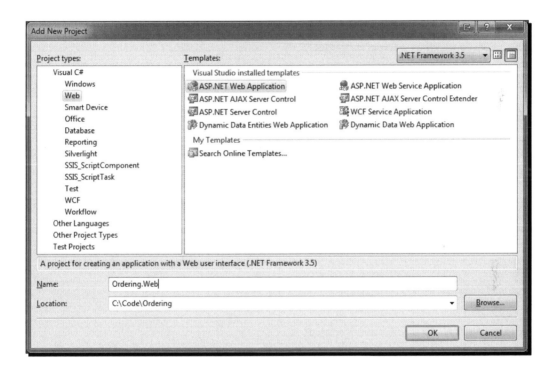

3. Right-click on the **Ordering.Web** project and select **Set as StartUp Project**, as shown in the following screenshot:

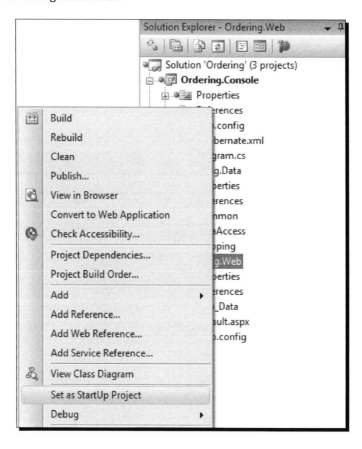

4. Right-click on the **Ordering.Web** project and select **Add Reference**, as shown in the following screenshot:

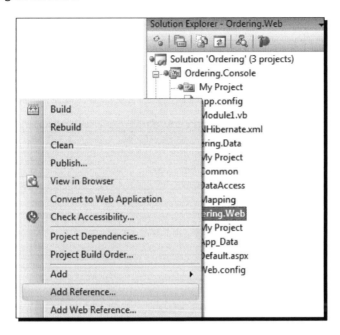

5. Click on the **Projects** tab, select the **Ordering.Data** project and then click on the **OK** button.

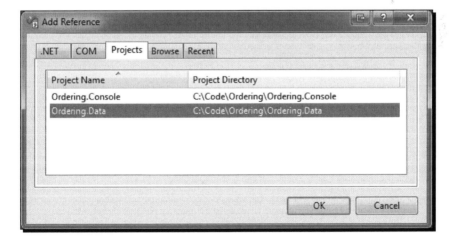

6. Open the `Web.config` file to add the sections for NHibernate and log4net. The easiest way to do this is to copy the sections from the `App.config` file in the `Ordering.Console` project. At the top of the file, between the `<configSections>` and `<sectionGroup>` tags, add the following hibernate-configuration and log4net configuration section blocks:

```
<section name="hibernate-configuration"
  type="NHibernate.Cfg.ConfigurationSectionHandler, NHibernate"/>
<section name="log4net"
  type="log4net.Config.Log4NetConfigurationSectionHandler,
  log4net"/>
```

7. Below the `</configSections>` section, add the `<hibernate-configuration>` and `<log4net>` configuration blocks:

```
<hibernate-configuration xmlns="urn:nhibernate-configuration-2.2">
  <session-factory>
    <property name="connection.provider">
      NHibernate.Connection.DriverConnectionProvider</property>
    <property name="dialect">
      NHibernate.Dialect.MsSql2008Dialect</property>
    <property name="connection.connection_string_name">
      Ordering
    </property>
    <property name="proxyfactory.factory_class">
      NHibernate.ByteCode.LinFu.ProxyFactoryFactory,
      NHibernate.ByteCode.LinFu
    </property>
    <mapping assembly="Ordering.Data"/>
  </session-factory>
</hibernate-configuration>
<log4net>
  <appender name="Console"
    type="log4net.Appender.ConsoleAppender">
    <layout type="log4net.Layout.PatternLayout">
      <conversionPattern value="%d{HH:mm:ss.fff}
        [%t] %p %c - %m%n"/>
    </layout>
  </appender>
  <appender name="RollingLogFile"
    type="log4net.Appender.RollingFileAppender">
    <threshold value="DEBUG" />
    <file value="logfile" />
    <appendToFile value="true" />
    <rollingStyle value="Date" />
    <datePattern value="yyyy-MM-dd'.log'" />
    <staticLogFileName value="false" />
    <layout type="log4net.Layout.PatternLayout">
```

```
        <conversionPattern value="%date [%thread] %-5level %logger
          [%property{NDC}] - %message%newline" />
      </layout>
    </appender>

    <!-- levels: ALL, DEBUG, INFO, WARN, ERROR, FATAL, OFF -->
    <root>
      <priority value="ALL"/>
      <appender-ref ref="RollingLogFile"/>
    </root>
    <logger name="Audit" additivity="false">
      <appender-ref ref="Console"/>
    </logger>
</log4net>
```

8. Replace the `<connectionStrings/>` block with our `<connectionStrings>` section:

```
<connectionStrings>
  <add name="Ordering"
    connectionString="Server=(local)\SQLExpress;
    Database=ordering;Trusted_Connection=true;" />
</connectionStrings>
```

9. Press *F5* or select **Debug | Start Debugging** to view our progress.

If you get a pop-up window as follows, select **Modify the Web.config file to enable debug**, which will change the `<compilation>` tag in the `<system.web>` section of the `Web.config` file to read: `<compilation debug="true">`. In VB.NET, the line will read: `<compilation debug="true" strict="false" explicit="true">`.

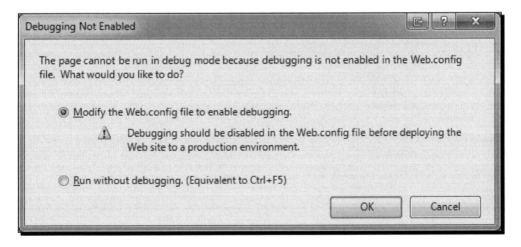

Remember to set the debug flag to `false` before you compile your web project for production. If the compilation tag has `debug="true"`, then the application will contain information that could make it easier for an attacker to plan an attack to compromise your site or its users.

10. When your browser starts, it should display an empty web page, as shown in the following screenshot. This is because we haven't added any content to our web application yet.

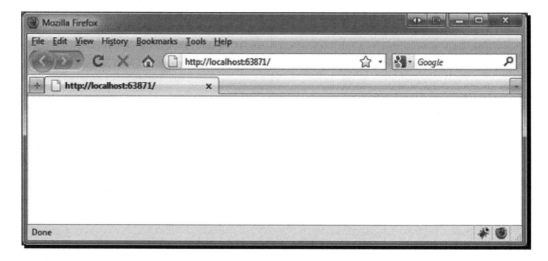

What just happened?

Now that we have a working ASP.NET web application project, we are ready to create some data bound controls.

Basic data binding techniques

There are a few simple techniques you will need to employ to make data binding work. The basic items we will need are a source of data, some data items to bind, and a control that allows data binding.

Essentially, a Data Source is an instance or a collection of instances that we will use to populate our control(s). For instance, if we had a group of products, we could create an IList of classes containing image and product name, size, weight, price, and so on.

There are two common ways to set the `DataSource` property of a control. The first is to directly bind it from the code behind or within another object. The second is to use a `DataSourceId` to specify the ID of a control on the page such as an `ObjectDataSource` control from which the data is coming.

The individual data items that make up the Data Source can be just about anything, from a simple string to a full-blown POCO with properties of child POCOs.

There are several controls that allow data binding, such as the DataGrid, ListView, Repeater, DataList, and even a Textbox or Label. These controls will bind in one of two ways, namely, simple or complex data binding.

With simple data binding, we can bind a single data item property, such as `Image`, to a property of the control, `Text` for example. In ASP.NET, this could look something like as follows:

```
<asp:TextBox Text='<%# Eval("Image") %>' runat="server" />
```

Complex binding allows us to bind one or more properties of the Data Source to one or more properties of the control. This works well for collections of records, even if a collection only contains one record. An example of complex binding would be a GridView, which renders a spreadsheet-type grid or table for the bound data:

```
<asp:GridView ID="productGrid" AutoGenerateColumns="false"
  runat="server">
  <Columns>
    <asp:ImageField DataImageUrlField="Image"
      DataAlternateTextField="ProductName" />
    <asp:BoundField DataField="ProductName" HeaderText="Product" />
  </Columns>
</asp:GridView>
```

For each record bound to the DataSource property of the control, a new row will be generated. In the case of the GridView just mentioned, it will generate an image (`<img>`) tag containing the URL to the product image and a second column containing the product name. It will also have a header on the ProductName column, with the title **Product**. It should look as shown in the following screenshot:

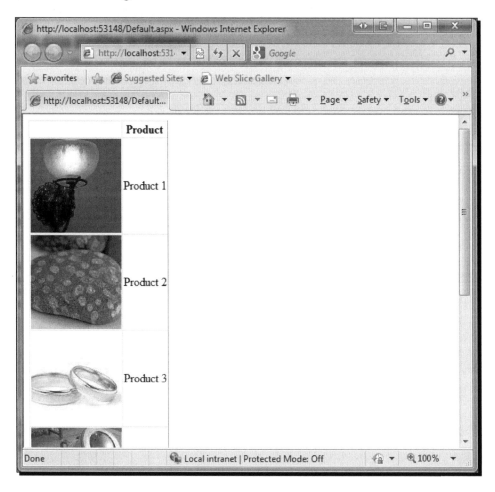

Common data binding methods

Each control has a primary way to bind data to it, and they generally fall into two categories, namely, directly bound and templated. A directly-bound control uses individual fields, such as the `.Text` and `.Value` properties, or individual controls such as the `<asp:BoundField>` and `<asp:ImageField>` controls. A couple of simple examples of this type of control, besides the GridView control, are the `<asp:DropDownList>` and `<asp:CheckBoxList>`.

The `<asp:DropDownList>` exposes the properties `DataSource`, `DataTextField`, and `DataValueField`. By setting these properties, either in the ASPX page or the code behind, our data will be bound to the control. The ASPX code for this control would be something like as follows:

```
<asp:DropDownList ID="productDropDownList"
   DataTextField="ProductName"
   DataValueField="Image" runat="server" />
```

When we view the page with a browser, the control that gets generated is as follows:

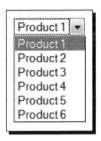

The `<asp:CheckBoxList>` also exposes the properties `DataSource`, `DataTextField`, and `DataValueField`. The ASPX code for this control would be something like as follows:

```
<asp:CheckBoxList ID="productDropDownList"
   DataTextField="ProductName"
   DataValueField="Image" runat="server" />
```

When we view the page with a browser, the control that gets generated is as follows:

When we use a templated control, we specify what the resulting ASPX page should look like. We create a basic layout for each of the data items and the control renders them when it binds the data.

When we create the layout, we need to display our data within that layout. We can do this a number of ways, but the simplest has to be the `Eval("PropertyName")` method. To display the data, you simply tell the `Eval()` method the name of the property in the DataSource that it should display and it substitutes that data for the placeholder. The basic ASP.NET code is as follows:

```
<%# Eval("PropertyName") %>
```

If we wanted to bind the `Image` field of our DataSource to the `ImageUrl` property of an `<asp:Image>` control, we can use the syntax as follows:

```
<asp:Image ImageUrl='<%# Eval("Image") %>' runat="server" />
```

If we want to change the format of the data, we can use the standard string formatting methods that we use with the `string.Format()` method. For example, if we need to prepend `~/Images/` to our `Image` property, we can call:

```
DataBinder.Eval(Container.DataItem, "Image", "~/Images/{0}")
```

This will replace the `{0}` placeholder with the data in the `Image` property, resulting in a string of `~/Images/product1.jpg`.

One thing to keep in mind when you are data binding is that not all the data that you bind will be safe. Unsavory characters or even normal users may add content through your web forms or other processes that would render unsafe information to browsers that render your content.

One attack of this type is called **Cross-site Scripting (XSS)** and it's a big problem for applications that present user or third-party data. Make sure that you use the proper encoding (`Server.HTMLEncode`, `Server.URLEncode`, and so on) or use the Microsoft Anti-Cross Site Scripting Library methods to perform this task. (`http://msdn.microsoft.com/en-us/security/ee658075.aspx`).

To view this in action, all you have to do is put the following code into the "ProductName" of one of our products:

```
<script>alert('XSS');
</script>
```

When we render this data, the browser will show an alert box with the message "XSS".

We can protect the data in our previous repeater control by simply URLEncoding the Image and HTMLEncoding the ProductName, like this:

```
<asp:Image ImageUrl='<%# Server.UrlEncode
  (Eval("Image").ToString()) %>' runat="server" />
<br />
<%# Server.HtmlEncode(Eval("ProductName").ToString())
%><br />
```

One thing to note: `Server.HtmlEncode` will not necessarily protect you from all script attacks; you will need to be aware of what context your data is being written to.

The Anti-Cross Site Scripting Library has more methods to protect this data, such as the `AntiXss.JavascriptEncode` method.

A simple templated control

One of the simplest templated controls has to be the `<asp:Repeater>` control. You give it an `<ItemTemplate>`, provide data, and it renders. It doesn't get much simpler than that! An example of the `<asp:Repeater>` control in action would be something like the following:

```
<asp:Repeater ID="productRepeater" runat="server">
  <ItemTemplate>
    <asp:Image ImageUrl='<%# Eval("Image") %>' runat="server" />
    <br />

    <%# Eval("ProductName") %><br />
  </ItemTemplate>
</asp:Repeater>
```

By using the `<%# Eval() %>` syntax, we set various properties of the controls or render the text to the website.

Pop quiz – basic data binding

1. Which controls provide the most flexibility over layout and design?

    a. Templated controls

    b. Directly-bound controls

    c. Simple controls

    d. They're all the same

2. How do we bind data to a templated control?

    a. `DataSource` property

    b. `DataSourceID` property

    c. From another object

    d. Templated controls cannot display data

3. How can we define the data that we want a templated control to display?

    a. `<%# Eval("PropertyName") %>`

    b. `<%# PropertyName %>`

    c. `<%# Response.Write("PropertyName") %>`

    d. Templated controls cannot display data

Creating a control instance

Many of the CSS templates "in the wild" use lists and reorganize them with CSS so they are displayed in the way the designer intended. Instead of generating a table with three columns and having to manually manipulate the data into those columns, we can use CSS to lay out the data.

Consider the following table structure to lay out our products:

```
<table>
  <tr>
    <td><img src="Images/product1.jpg" /></td>
    <td><img src="Images/product2.jpg" /></td>
    <td><img src="Images/product3.jpg" /></td>
  </tr>
  <tr>
    <td>Product  1</td>
    <td>Product  2</td>
    <td>Product  3</td>
  </tr>
  <tr>
    <td><img src="Images/product4.jpg" /></td>
    <td><img src="Images/product5.jpg" /></td>
    <td><img src="Images/product6.jpg" /></td>
  </tr>
  <tr>
    <td>Product  4</td>
    <td>Product  5</td>
    <td>Product  6</td>
  </tr>
</table>
```

While this layout would definitely present our products to our user, it has a few limitations. First, it's pretty "heavy", in other words, it makes the browser work harder than a CSS layout does to generate all of the tables and rows. Also, it takes more logic to make it work if you only have a number of products that aren't readily divisible by three. Lastly, and probably most importantly, it's much more difficult for the webmaster (you) to maintain and keep straight.

With an **Unordered List (UL)**, some **List Items (LI)**, and a simple block of CSS code, we can make our products "flow" neatly into columns.

```
.products li
{
  Display: inline;
  float: left;
  Margin: 0 0 15px 15px;
}
```

Now, if we create an unordered list (UL) that contains our products, they will lay out in nice neat columns:

```
<ul class="products">
    <li><img src="Images/product1.jpg" /><br />Product 1</li>
    <li><img src="Images/product2.jpg" /><br />Product 2</li>
    <li><img src="Images/product3.jpg" /><br />Product 3</li>
    <li><img src="Images/product4.jpg" /><br />Product 4</li>
    <li><img src="Images/product5.jpg" /><br />Product 5</li>
    <li><img src="Images/product6.jpg" /><br />Product 6</li>
</ul>
```

If we look at this code in the browser, it will look like this:

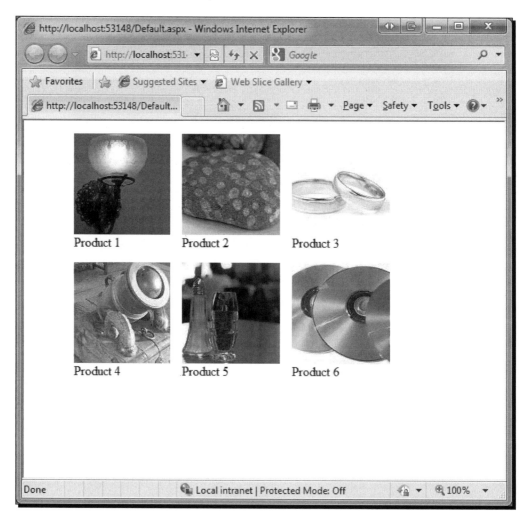

The nice thing about this CSS is that if we resize the browser window, the products will automatically rearrange themselves to fit in the window.

The <asp:ListView> control

The first thing we need to do to see some data binding in action is to add a control that can actually take advantage of it. One of the simplest and most versatile controls to use has to be the new <asp:ListView> control in ASP.NET 3.5.

The <asp:ListView> control has a few nice features that make it ideal for data binding, especially in the dynamic web world with JavaScript and CSS. One of these features is the <LayoutTemplate> block, which lets you specify a "wrapper" for the generated data.

If you're not quite sure what that means, it simply means that we want to create a set of tags to "wrap" our data. This could be the <ul> tags for our <li> data items, a set of <div> or <table> tags, or any other code.

In order to get the <LayoutTemplate> to generate the same code we created earlier, we just need to add in our <ul> tags with the class declaration, and an <asp:PlaceHolder> with the ID of itemPlaceHolder and a runat="server", as shown in the following code snippet:

```
<LayoutTemplate>
  <ul class="products">
    <asp:PlaceHolder ID="itemPlaceholder" runat="server" />
  </ul>
</LayoutTemplate>
```

Then, to create the <li> product data, we just create an <ItemTemplate> with our <asp:Image> and our text declaration:

```
<ItemTemplate>
  <li>
    <asp:Image ImageUrl='<%# Eval("Image") %>' runat="server" />
    <br />
    <%# Eval("ProductName") %>
  </li>
</ItemTemplate>
```

Another great feature of the <asp:ListView> control is the <EmptyDataTemplate>. We can set some default code for the control to display if there are no records to display.

```
<EmptyDataTemplate>
  <div>
    No products were found
  </div>
</EmptyDataTemplate>
```

With all the code together, the `<asp:ListView>` control would look as follows:

```
<asp:ListView ID="productList" runat="server">
  <LayoutTemplate>
    <ul class="products">
      <asp:PlaceHolder ID="itemPlaceholder" runat="server" />
    </ul>
  </LayoutTemplate>
  <ItemTemplate>
    <li>
      <asp:Image ImageUrl='<%# Eval("Image") %>' runat="server" />
      <br /><%# Eval("ProductName") %>
    </li>
  </ItemTemplate>
  <EmptyDataTemplate>
    <div>
      No products were found
    </div>
  </EmptyDataTemplate>
</asp:ListView>
```

The `<asp:ObjectDataSource>` control

A great way to work with NHibernate data and data-bound controls is to populate the controls with an `<asp:ObjectDataSource>`. This control allows you to specify what type of objects the control will return (`DataObjectTypeName`) and what object the control will need to access to perform the CRUD operations (`TypeName`).

The basic `<asp:ObjectDataSource>` control just needs four things to get it going, namely, an ID, a DataObjectTypeName (POCO), a Type Name (Data Access Object), and a CRUD method (Create, Read, Update, and Delete). A sample `<asp:ObjectDataSource>` to retrieve all of the OrderHeader items in the database would look like this:

```
<asp:ObjectDataSource ID="orderHeaderSource"
  DataObjectTypeName="Ordering.Data.OrderHeader"
  TypeName="Ordering.Data.DataAccess.OrderHeaderDataControl"
  SelectMethod="GetAll" runat="server">
</asp:ObjectDataSource>
```

Now that we have the ID (`orderHeaderSource`), we can use it in any data-bound control with a `DataSourceID` property! This includes `<asp:Repeater>`, `<asp:ListView>`, `<asp:GridView>`, `<asp:FormView>`, and so on.

So, you say, this is great if I want to get ALL the records but what about calling other methods on the DataAccessControl? No problem.

Let's say that we wanted to get an `OrderHeader` with the ID of "1". Remember our `OrderHeaderDataControl` has a method `GetById` that is as follows:

```
public OrderHeader GetById(int Id)
{
  return Session.Get<OrderHeader>(Id);
}
```

All we have to do is change the `SelectMethod` to `GetById` and pass in the number "1". We can do this with a `SelectParameter`.

The parameters for the Select, Insert, Update, and Delete methods are specified in blocks between the start and end `<asp:ObjectDataSource>` tags. To specify a static parameter of `Id` with the value of "1", we can just declare it as follows:

```
<SelectParameters>
  <asp:Parameter Name="Id" Type="Int32" DefaultValue="1" />
</SelectParameters>
```

Now our `<asp:ObjectDataSource>` will call the `GetById` method and pass in the number "1" to the "Id" property.

What if we want the parameter to come from a `QueryString` variable called `OrderHeaderId`? We just change the `<asp:Parameter>` to an `<asp:QueryStringParameter>` as follows:

```
<asp:QueryStringParameter Name="Id" Type="Int32"
  QueryStringField="OrderHeaderId" />
```

If we wanted the parameter to come from a Session variable called "CurrentOrderId"?

```
<asp:SessionParameter Name="Id" Type="Int32"
  SessionField="CurrentOrderId" />
```

The possibilities are virtually endless. To specify multiple parameters to a method, all you have to do is add multiple `<asp:XParameter>` controls, and ASP.NET will figure out which method to call, based on the number and types of the parameters that you specify.

Take a look at this fully-populated `OrderHeader` `<asp: ObjectDataSource>` control to get an idea of what is possible:

```
<asp:ObjectDataSource ID="OrderHeaderDetailSource"
  SelectMethod="GetById" InsertMethod="Save"
  UpdateMethod="Save" DeleteMethod="Delete" DataObjectTypeName="
  Ordering.Data.OrderHeader"
  TypeName=" Ordering.Data.DataAccess.OrderHeaderDataControl"
  runat="server">
  <SelectParameters>
```

```
    <asp:QueryStringParameter Name="id"
      QueryStringField="OrderHeaderId" Type="Int32" />
  </SelectParameters>
  <InsertParameters>
    <asp:Parameter Name="orderHeader" Type="Object" />
    <asp:Parameter Direction="Output" Name="id" Type="Object" />
  </InsertParameters>
  <UpdateParameters>
    <asp:Parameter Name="orderHeader" Type="Object" />
    <asp:Parameter Direction="Output" Name="id" Type="Object" />
  </UpdateParameters>
  <DeleteParameters>
    <asp:Parameter Name="orderHeader" Type="Object" />
  </DeleteParameters>
</asp:ObjectDataSource>
```

Time for action – adding our first data bound control

Now we can add some data-bound controls to the web application project we created earlier, and really see the power of NHibernate and ASP.NET together.

1. Open up the `Default.aspx` page from the Ordering.Web solution we created earlier. In the `<head>` section, between the `</title>` tag and the `</head>` tag, add the following CSS code to properly render our items:

```
<style type="text/css">
  .contacts li
  {
    display: inline;
    float: left;
    margin: 0 0 15px 15px;
  }
</style>
```

2. Inside the body, between the `<div>` and `</div>` tags, add the following code:

```
<asp:ListView ID="contactView" runat="server">
</asp:ListView>
```

3. If you look down at the bottom of the screen, you will see three buttons, **Design**, **Split**, and **Source**. Select the **Split** button to split the page into two parts, one displaying the code and the other displaying the "real-time view" of your page.

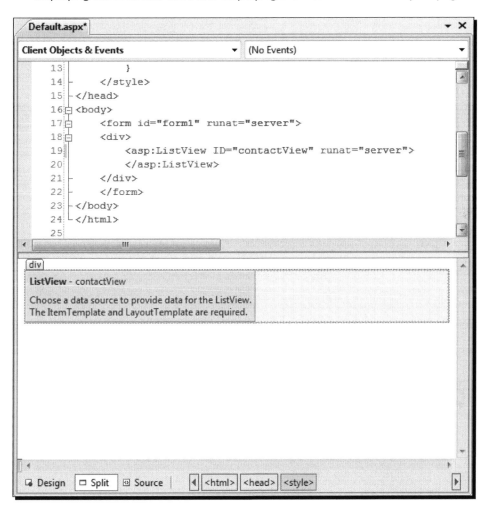

4. As you can see in the **Design** portion of the screen, our control needs an `<ItemTemplate>` and a `<LayoutTemplate>`. We'll start off by adding the `<LayoutTemplate>` to create our `<ul>` tags and adding the placeholder for the Data Items. Between the opening and closing `<asp:ListView>` tags, add the following code:

```
<LayoutTemplate>
  <ul class="contacts">
    <asp:PlaceHolder ID="itemPlaceholder" runat="server" />
  </ul>
</LayoutTemplate>
```

5. The next thing we need to add is the actual `<ItemTemplate>` block, which will fill into our `<asp:PlaceHolder>` control named ItemPlaceHolder in the `<LayoutTemplate>` block. Add the following code to bind the Last Name and First Name with a comma between them:

```
<ItemTemplate>
  <li>
    <p>
      <%# Eval("LastName") %>, <%# Eval("FirstName") %>
    </p>
  </li>
</ItemTemplate>
```

6. At this point, it would be nice to see if what we have is working. Let's add some data to our page so we can test it out. Add the following `<asp:ObjectDataSource>` code to tell NHibernate to get some data for us:

```
<asp:ObjectDataSource ID="contactSource"
  DataObjectTypeName="Ordering.Data.Contact"
  TypeName="Ordering.Data.DataAccess.ContactDataControl"
  SelectMethod="GetAll" runat="server">
</asp:ObjectDataSource>
```

7. The last thing we have to do to make it work is tell our `<asp:ListView>` control to use our `<asp:ObjectDataSource>`. In the opening of the tag, add the following code:

```
DataSourceID="contactSource"
```

So, your final `<asp:ListView>` tag should look as follows:

```
<asp:ListView ID="contactView" DataSourceID="contactSource"
  runat="server">
```

8. Press *F5* or select **Debug | Start Debugging** to view our progress. You should get something similar to the following screenshot:

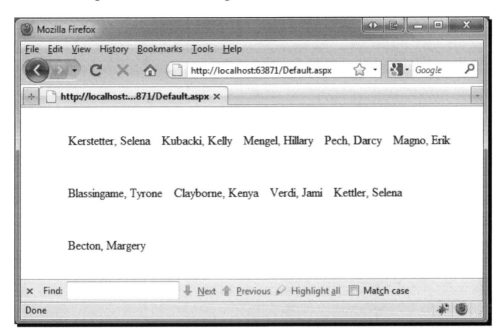

If you run into trouble, then take a look at your `<asp:ObjectDataSource>` control. Most likely it's an issue with your `DataObjectTypeName` (POCO) or the `TypeName` (Data Access Control) namespaces.

Take a look at your object and see what the namespace is, and adjust the `DataObjectTypeName` or `TypeName` to match the full names of the actual POCO or DAO classes.

Your TypeName will be `Ordering.Data.DataAccess.ContactDataControl` if your `ContactDataControl` is as follows:

```
namespace Ordering.Data.DataAccess
{
    public class ContactDataControl
```

However, if your `ContactDataControl` doesn't have any namespace wrapper, such as `Public Class ContactDataControl`, then the TypeName will just be the name of the project and the name of the class or `Ordering.Data.ContactDataControl`.

9. Now that we have some basic data-bound controls, let's get a little trickier. Let's add another control inside our `<li>` tags such as the `<asp:HyperLink>` control. We will bind the `Text` property of the control to the `Email` property of the Data Item. We will bind the `NavigateUrl` property to a formatted string, "mailto:{0}?subje ct=NHibernate&body=Hello from NHibernate", filling in the `{0}` with the `Email` property. Add the following code after the `<%# Eval("FirstName") %>` tag, but before the `</p>`:

```
<br />
<asp:HyperLink NavigateUrl='<%# DataBinder.Eval(
  Container.DataItem,"Email",
  "mailto:{0}?subject=NHibernate&body=Hello from NHibernate") %>'
  Text='<%# Eval("Email") %>' runat="server" />
```

10. Now if we run the code, we will have a hyperlink under each of our contacts that has an e-mail address, as shown in the following screenshot:

If we click on one of the links, it will start our default e-mail handler and pre-fill the address, subject, and body for us, as shown in the following screenshot:

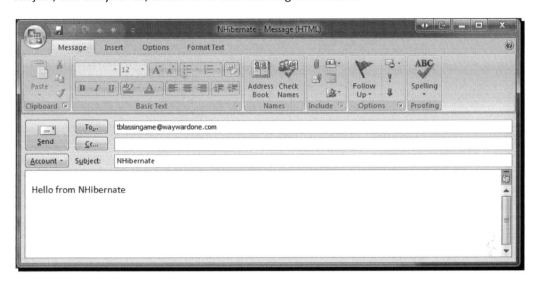

11. The last thing we should do is add an `<EmptyDataTemplate>`, in case our data control doesn't return any data. After the `<ItemTemplate>` block, add the following block of code:

```
<EmptyDataTemplate>
  <div>
    No contacts were found
  </div>
</EmptyDataTemplate>
```

12. Our completed code should look as follows:

```
<body>
  <form id="form1" runat="server">
    <div>
      <asp:ListView ID="contactView" DataSourceID="contactSource"
        runat="server">
        <LayoutTemplate>
          <ul class="contacts">
            <asp:PlaceHolder ID="itemPlaceholder"
              runat="server" />
          </ul>
        </LayoutTemplate>
        <ItemTemplate>
          <li>
            <p>
```

```
       <%# Eval("LastName") %>, 
       <%# Eval("FirstName") %>
       <br />
       <asp:HyperLink NavigateUrl='<%# DataBinder.Eval
         (Container.DataItem,"Email","mailto:
         {0}?subject=NHibernate&body=Hello from
         NHibernate") %>' Text='<%# Eval("Email") %>'
         runat="server" />
      </p>
     </li>
   </ItemTemplate>
   <EmptyDataTemplate>
     <div>
       No contacts were found
     </div>
   </EmptyDataTemplate>
  </asp:ListView>
  <asp:ObjectDataSource ID="contactSource"
    DataObjectTypeName="Ordering.Data.Contact"
    TypeName="Ordering.Data.DataAccess.ContactDataControl"
    SelectMethod="GetAll" runat="server">
  </asp:ObjectDataSource>
 </div>
 </form>
</body>
```

What just happened?

With just a few lines of ASP.NET code (and no code-behind), we have created a complete CSS-driven, data-bound web page that displays contacts in a neatly formatted columnar layout.

Direct data binding

The easiest (though probably hardest to maintain) method to bind data to controls is to retrieve the data in the code behind and set it to the DataSource property of the control.

To make the <asp:ListView> from the previous section work, we can knock up a quick Products class:

```
public Products(string Image, string ProductName)
{
  this.Image = Image;
  this.ProductName = ProductName;
}
public string Image { get; set; }
public string ProductName { get; set; }
```

Next, we just need to create a few instances of the `Products` class inside the `Page_Load` method:

```
IList<Products> products = new List<Products>();
products.Add(new Products("Images/product1.jpg", "Product 1"));
products.Add(new Products("Images/product2.jpg", "Product 2"));
products.Add(new Products("Images/product3.jpg", "Product 3"));
products.Add(new Products("Images/product4.jpg", "Product 4"));
products.Add(new Products("Images/product5.jpg", "Product 5"));
products.Add(new Products("Images/product6.jpg", "Product 6"));
```

And finally, we set the `DataSource` of the control to our list of products and call `DataBind()`, as shown in the following lines of code:

```
productList.DataSource = products;
this.DataBind();
```

VOILA! We have a data-bound list of products that displays using CSS exactly like our original list.

There are two major problems with binding data this way:

- ◆ Your data retrieval and storage code is visibly separated from your display.
- ◆ You have to do all of the data "munging" yourself, that is, taking the data from the control and saving it, binding the data to the control, updating it when it changes, and so on.

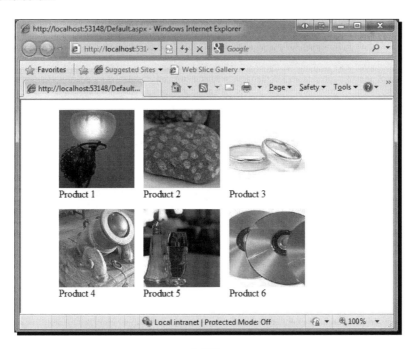

In the code that we created earlier, remove the `DataSourceID` property from the `<asp:ListView>` control and create your own `IList<Contact>`, either manually or by retrieving them from the database using one of the methods on the `Ordering.Data.DataAccess.ContactDataControl`. Populate the `<asp:ListView>` by setting your `IList<Contact>` to the `DataSource` property of the `<asp:ListView>` and calling `this.DataBind()`.

One last control—the <asp:FormView>

One of the easiest ways to add data manipulation to a .NET application is to use the `<asp:FormView>` control. This control is a templated control, with templates for `<ItemTemplate>` (ReadOnly view), `<InsertItemTemplate>` (Insert), `<EditItemTemplate>` (Edit), and `<EmptyDataTemplate>`.

The following code snippet shows the basic syntax of the control, which is similar to the others that we have implemented:

```
<asp:FormView ID="contactFormView" DataSourceID="contactDetailSource"
DataKeyNames="Id" runat="server">

</asp:FormView>
```

One property, which is of particular interest to us, that this control exposes is the `DataKeyNames` property. By setting this property, we tell the control the name of the Primary Key field or fields (separated by a comma) that make a unique record. To set this property for our objects, we just need to say:

```
DataKeyNames="Id"
```

As with all templated controls, we can use CSS to "spruce up" the look of our templates. Here is an example of using an HTML `<fieldset>` control with an ordered list (`<ol>`) to give us a nice look that is easy to skin:

```
<ItemTemplate>
  <fieldset>
    <legend>Contact Detail</legend>
    <ol>
      <li>
        <asp:Label ID="idLabel" Text="Id" runat="server" />
        <asp:Label ID="id" Text='<%# Eval("Id") %>'
          runat="server" />
      </li>
      <li>
        <asp:Label ID="lastNameLabel" Text='LastName'
          runat="server" />
```

```
        <asp:Label ID="lastName" Text='<%# Eval("LastName") %>'
          Enabled="false" runat="server" />
      </li>
      <li>
        <asp:Label ID="firstNameLabel" Text='FirstName'
          runat="server" />
        <asp:Label ID="firstName" Text='<%# Eval("FirstName") %>'
          Enabled="false"  runat="server" />
      </li>
      <li>
        <asp:Label ID="emailLabel" Text='Email' runat="server" />
        <asp:Label ID="email" Text='<%# Eval("Email") %>'
          Enabled="false" runat="server" />
      </li>
    </ol>
  </fieldset>
  <asp:Button ID="add" CommandName="New" Text="Add" runat="server" />
  <asp:Button ID="edit" CommandName="Edit" Text="Edit"
    runat="server" />
  <asp:Button ID="delete" CommandName="Delete" Text="Delete"
    runat="server" />
</ItemTemplate>
```

When we render this basic `<ItemTemplate>` bound to a `Contact` object, it will look similar to the following screenshot:

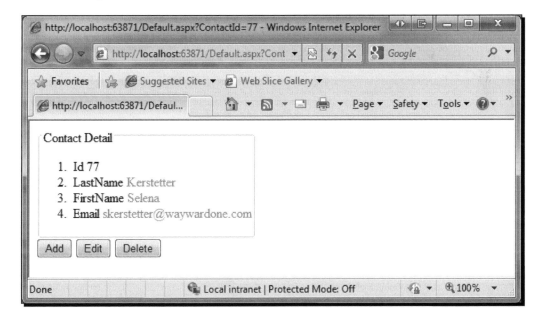

Notice in the `<ItemTemplate>` there is an `<asp:Button ID="edit">` with CommandName=`"Edit"`. The `<asp:FormView>` control will interpret these "CommandName" attributes and switch modes accordingly.

For example, when I click the button with the CommandName "Edit" specified, the control will display the `<EditItemTemplate>`, which we define as follows:

```
<EditItemTemplate>
  <fieldset>
    <legend>Edit Contact Detail</legend>
    <ol>
      <li>
        <asp:Label ID="idLabel" Text="Id" runat="server" />
        <asp:Label ID="id" Text='<%# Bind("Id") %>' runat="server" />
      </li>
      <li>
        <asp:Label ID="lastNameLabel" Text='LastName'
          runat="server" />
        <asp:TextBox ID="lastName" Text='<%# Bind("LastName") %>'
          runat="server" />
      </li>
      <li>
        <asp:Label ID="firstNameLabel" Text='FirstName'
          runat="server" />
        <asp:TextBox ID="firstName" Text='<%# Bind("FirstName") %>'
          runat="server" />
      </li>
      <li>
        <asp:Label ID="emailLabel" Text='Email' runat="server" />
        <asp:TextBox ID="email" Text='<%# Bind("Email") %>'
          runat="server" />
      </li>
    </ol>
  </fieldset>
  <asp:Button ID="submit" CommandName="Update" Text="Save"
    runat="server" />
</EditItemTemplate>
```

When we hit the **Edit** button, the browser will show something similar to the following screenshot:

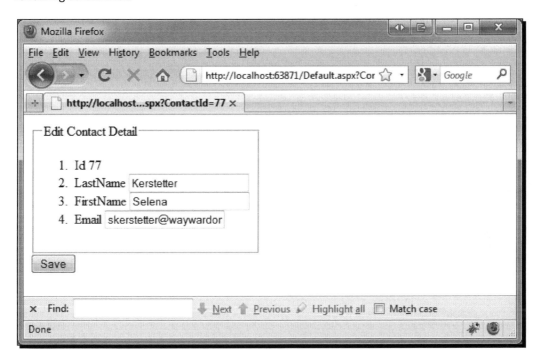

Similarly, when we hit the **Add** button, it will display the `<InsertItemTemplate>`, which is identical to the `<EditItemTemplate>`, except we remove the label for the "Id" because it is automatically assigned by NHibernate:

```
<InsertItemTemplate>
  <fieldset>
    <legend>New Contact Detail</legend>
    <ol>
      <li>
        <asp:Label ID="lastNameLabel" Text='LastName'
          runat="server" />
        <asp:TextBox ID="lastName" Text='<%# Bind("LastName") %>'
          runat="server" />
      </li>
      <li>
        <asp:Label ID="firstNameLabel" Text='FirstName'
          runat="server" />
        <asp:TextBox ID="firstName" Text='<%# Bind("FirstName") %>'
          runat="server" />
      </li>
```

```
    <li>
      <asp:Label ID="emailLabel" Text='Email' runat="server" />
      <asp:TextBox ID="email" Text='<%# Bind("Email") %>'
        runat="server" />
    </li>
  </ol>
</fieldset>
<asp:Button ID="submit" CommandName="Insert" Text="Save"
  runat="server" />
</InsertItemTemplate>
```

The last template we need to view is the `<EmptyDataTemplate>`, which simply tells us that there are no records and presents the "Add" button for us to insert a new record:

```
<EmptyDataTemplate>
  <fieldset>
    <legend>Contact Detail</legend>No Record Selected
  </fieldset>
  <asp:Button ID="add" CommandName="New" Text="Add" runat="server" />
</EmptyDataTemplate>
```

The only thing left is to define an `<asp:ObjectDataSource>` to populate and perform the CRUD operations for us:

```
<asp:ObjectDataSource ID="contactDetailSource" SelectMethod="GetById"
  InsertMethod="Save" UpdateMethod="Save" DeleteMethod="Delete"
  DataObjectTypeName="Ordering.Data.Contact"
  TypeName="Ordering.Data.DataAccess.ContactDataControl"
  runat="server">
  <SelectParameters>
    <asp:QueryStringParameter Name="id" QueryStringField="ContactId"
      Type="Int32" />
  </SelectParameters>
  <InsertParameters>
    <asp:Parameter Name="contact" Type="Object" />
    <asp:Parameter Direction="Output" Name="id" Type="Object" />
  </InsertParameters>
  <UpdateParameters>
    <asp:Parameter Name="contact" Type="Object" />
    <asp:Parameter Direction="Output" Name="id" Type="Object" />
  </UpdateParameters>
  <DeleteParameters>
    <asp:Parameter Name="contact" Type="Object" />
  </DeleteParameters>
</asp:ObjectDataSource>
```

With no record specified, the control will look as shown in the following screenshot:

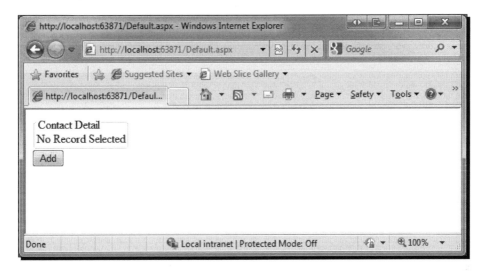

Have a go hero – creating an <asp:FormView>

Now that we have the basis for inserting and updating data, have a crack at creating an `<asp:FormView>` to insert, update, edit, and delete Contacts. Try applying a little CSS to make your blocks more visually appealing.

Summary

In this chapter, we learned a lot about data binding in ASP.NET and how to make both templated and non-templated controls work with data binding.

Specifically, we covered:

- Data Binding techniques in an ASP.NET project
- Using the `<asp:ListView>` control
- Performing CRUD operations using the `<asp:ObjectDataSource>` control
- Directly Binding Data to ASP.NET controls
- Using the `<asp:GridView>` control
- Binding data to `<asp:Repeater>` and `<asp:DataList>` controls
- Databinding with `<asp:DropDownList>` and `<asp:CheckBoxList>` controls
- Using the `<asp:FormView>` control to manage data

Now that we've learned about data binding, we're ready to talk about the .NET Security provider model, which is the topic of the next chapter.

10
.NET Security

ASP.NET has several controls and providers that make securing ASP.NET applications much simpler. Using NHibernate, we can implement two of these—the membership and role providers—and use all of the standard security controls to secure access to some of our pages. We will also talk about some basic Internet security items to help you protect yourself and your users.

In this chapter, we will discuss:

- ◆ Built-in controls
    - ❏ `<asp:Login>`
    - ❏ `<asp:LoginStatus>`
    - ❏ `<asp:LoginView>`
- ◆ Membership provider
- ◆ `Web.config` location security
- ◆ Role provider
- ◆ Configuration

Let's jump right in.

Built-in controls

Two of the controls you will need to get familiar with, if you are going to do security on your site, are the `<asp:Login>` and the `<asp:LoginStatus>` controls to show the login and status to our users. These controls, along with the forms authentication model, provide a basic foundation for security in a .NET application.

The `<asp:Login>` control is a templated control like we discussed in *Chapter 9, Binding Data*. To add a login box, including Login and Password, to the page, we just need to add the `<asp:Login>` control to one of our pages.

```
<asp:Login ID="login" runat="server" />
```

With this simple line of code, our page will now render a login for us, ready to accept our login credentials, as shown in the following screenshot:

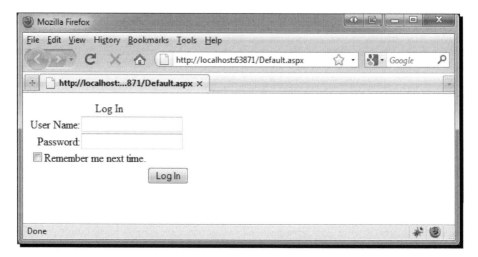

If we want our users to be directed to another page once they log in, we can add the `DestinationPageURL` property, which will redirect them once they log in:

```
DestinationPageURL="support.aspx"
```

I know what you're thinking: We said that this was a templated control, right? Well, it is. It just has a default template built in. If we want to override the template for the `<asp:Login>` control, all we have do is provide an alternate `<LayoutTemplate>` with a few controls. We need to have two textboxes, one with an ID of "UserName" and the second with an ID of "Password". We also need an `<asp:Button>` control with an ID of "Login" and a CommandName of "Login". We can also specify additional controls, such as a "RememberMe" checkbox, and so on.

```
<asp:Login ID="login" runat="server">
  <LayoutTemplate>
    Login: 
    <asp:TextBox ID="UserName" runat="server" />
    <br />
    Password: 
    <asp:TextBox ID="Password" runat="server" />
    <br />
```

```
        <asp:CheckBox ID="RememberMe" Text="Remember my login"
          runat="server" /><br />
        <asp:Button ID="Login" CommandName="Login" Text="Login"
          runat="server" />
    </LayoutTemplate>
  </asp:Login>
```

If we render this control, as specified here, it will look pretty similar to the original control template. Using this custom template, we can now use CSS to skin the control any way we want instead of having to use the default layout.

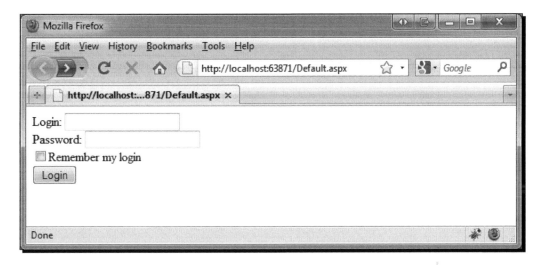

We should display the status of the user logged in somewhere, and give them a link to login and a link to log off. We can do all of this with an `<asp:LoginStatus>` control.

```
    <asp:LoginStatus ID="loginStatus" runat="server" />
```

 I like to stick an `<asp:LoginStatus>` control into my master page, so that I have a place for the user to log off on every page.

When it is rendered, the `<asp:LoginStatus>` control will just render a link, either **Login** or **Logout**, as shown in the following screenshot:

Time for action – adding a login to our page

If we are going to control user logins to our application, we first need to add the controls to our forms.

1. Open the `Ordering.Web` application we created earlier.

2. In the `Default.aspx` page, at the start inside the `<div>` tag, add the code for our `<asp:LoginStatus>` control:

    ```
    <asp:LoginStatus ID="loginStatus" runat="server" />
    ```

3. Let's add a break (`<br />`) tag after the `<asp:LoginStatus>` control to pretty it up a little:

    ```
    <asp:LoginStatus ID="loginStatus" runat="server" /><br />
    ```

4. Now we can add the `<asp:Login>` control to show our **User Name** and **Password** boxes:

    ```
    <asp:Login ID="login" runat="server" />
    ```

5. Pressing *F5* will bring up the page and show us our controls. It should look similar to the following screenshot:

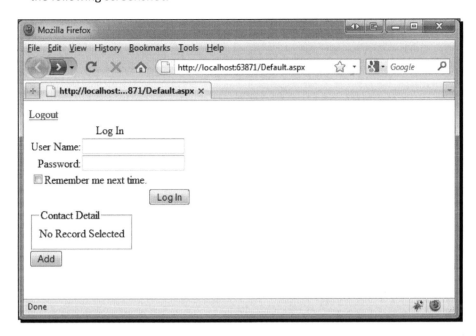

What just happened?

We just created login and status controls for our web application, and now we're ready to build the backend to actually make them work!

Membership providers

To make our login controls work with NHibernate, we need to implement the `System.Web.Security.MembershipProvider` abstract class. This is an abstract class specifically designed to allow us to implement the standard security model using our own authentication logic.

When we implement the abstract class, there are about 30 methods and properties that we can override to implement all of the features of the membership provider, but we really only have to implement one method to get it to work. If we implement the `ValidateUser()` method, we can have basic login functionality.

The `ValidateUser()` method has two parameters (both strings), `UserName` and `Password`. In our method, we need to accept these two parameters, validate that they match the credentials stored in the database, and return either `true` or `false` based on that validation.

A very simple implementation of the `ValidateUser()` method using NHibernate would be to simply hash the user-supplied password, retrieve the user record based on the `UserName`, and compare the passwords.

```
public override bool ValidateUser(string UserName, string Password)
{
  Login login = LoginDataControl.Instance.GetByUserName(UserName);
  if (login == null)
    return false;
  HMACSHA256 hash = new
    HMACSHA256(ASCIIEncoding.UTF8.GetBytes(login.Salt));
  string encodedPassword = Convert.ToBase64String
    (hash.ComputeHash(Encoding.Unicode.GetBytes(Password)));

  if (encodedPassword == login.Password && login.Active == true)
    return true;

  return false;
}
```

Notice that we pass in a byte[] key into the HMACSHA256 hashing algorithm. This is called a seed value, and it ensures that we will always get the same results back when we call `ComputeHash()`. If we didn't specify this key, then we would get different results every time because it would automatically generate a seed value.

While we can default this method to use hashing as the default password protection mechanism, the provider allows for many others. Some of the more common password protection providers are "Hashed", "Encrypted", and "Clear".

You shouldn't use "Clear" to store passwords in your database. Should the data ever be compromised, all of your users' passwords would be plainly visible to the attacker. A better method is to use hashed passwords and use a different key (salt) value for each user. You can store this salt value in the same record as the user because even if it is compromised, it would take an attacker a large amount of time to recompute each of the values.

Location security

One way to use our membership provider to control security is to add some configuration elements in the `Web.config` file. We can use the `<location>` element to specify the name of a directory or a page, and then use an `<authorization>` block to control access.

The `<location>` element is specified in the `Web.config` file, usually right after the `</system.web>` element as part of the `<configuration>` block. To control security, we have two major options, namely, "allow" and "deny". We can also specify if we want the security to apply to everyone (*), only anonymous users (?), or to specific users or roles.

If you look at the following `<location>` element, you will see that we are denying access to all unauthenticated (anonymous) users, that is, we only allow logged-in users to visit the `SecurePage.aspx` page.

```
<location path="/SecurePage.aspx">
  <system.web>
    <authorization>
      <deny users="?"/>
    </authorization>
  </system.web>
</location>
```

If you look at the following `<location>` element, you will see that we are denying access to all users except those with `Administrator` and `DataAdmin` roles.

```
<location path="/SecurePage.aspx">
  <system.web>
    <authorization>
      <allow roles="Administrator"/>
      <allow roles="DataAdmin"/>
      <deny users="*"/>
    </authorization>
  </system.web>
</location>
```

More information on ASP.NET Authorization is available on the MSDN site at `http://msdn.microsoft.com/en-us/library/aa719554%28VS.71%29.aspx`.

Pop quiz – doing the thing

1. Which of the following means "All Users"?

    a. ?

    b. *

    c. &

    d. None of the above

2. Which of these allows us to control authentication?

    a. `<location>`

    b. Users, roles

    c. allow, deny

    d. All of the above

3. In the following block, who will have access to the `Default.aspx` page in the root folder?

```
<location path=".">
  <system.web>
    <authorization>
      <deny users="?"/>
    </authorization>
  </system.web>
</location>
```

    a. No one

    b. All logged-in users

    c. Only anonymous users

    d. Impossible to tell

Configuring our provider

Once our providers are written, we need to let ASP.NET know that we are going to use them. The first thing we need to do is go into the `Web.config` and change the authentication method in the `system.web` section from `Windows` to `Forms`. To do this, we literally just change the value to `Forms` as follows:

```
<authentication mode="Forms"/>
```

One thing we should also specify here is the URL of the login page in case our user tries to go to a secure page without being logged in (that is, from a bookmark). We can use the `loginUrl` property of the `forms` tag to handle this as follows:

```
<authentication mode="Forms">
  <forms loginUrl="~/Login.aspx"/>
</authentication>
```

Next, we need to add a configuration block to define the membership provider. This is done using the `<membership>` block and a `<providers>` block to actually define the provider itself.

The `<membership>` block has a parameter `defaultProvider` where you can provide the name of the default provider for it to use. A sample configuration would look something as follows:

```
<membership defaultProvider="OrderingMembershipProvider">
  <providers>
    <add name="OrderingMembershipProvider"
      type="Ordering.Data.OrderingMembershipProvider,
      Ordering.Data" />
  </providers>
</membership>
```

You will notice that the provider construct is very similar to the `<connection strings>` or the `<app settings>` blocks within the `web.config` or `app.config` file. It simply uses the add notation, with a `name` (for use with the `defaultProvider` name, and so on) and a `type` parameter denoting where .NET should look for the code.

There are numerous settings for this provider block such as encryption, validation keys (salt values), whether or not password resets are enabled, and so on, but this is all that is needed to get it up and running.

Time for action – create a membership provider

Let's add the membership provider to our code and configure our application to use it.

1. Before we get started, we will need a place to store our new logins in the database. Execute the following SQL to create the "Login" table in our "Ordering" database with SQL Server Management Studio (SSMS):

```
CREATE TABLE [dbo].[Login](
    [Id] [int] IDENTITY(1,1) NOT NULL,
    [Active] [bit] NOT NULL,
    [Email] [varchar](255) NULL,
    [FirstName] [varchar](255) NULL,
    [LastName] [varchar](255) NULL,
    [UserName] [varchar](255) NOT NULL,
    [Password] [varchar](255) NOT NULL,
    [PasswordQuestion] [varchar](255) NULL,
    [PasswordAnswer] [varchar](255) NULL,
    [Salt] [varchar](255) NOT NULL,
    CONSTRAINT [PK_Login] PRIMARY KEY CLUSTERED
    (
        [Id] ASC
    )
)
```

2. Now you will need to create a Login POCO, a Login Data Control (DAO), and add the XML mapping files. Refer to the previous chapters if you need a little help.

3. Add a new class to the `Ordering.Data` project called `OrderingMembershipProvider`.

4. Add a reference to `System.Configuration` and `System.Web` as shown in the following screenshot:

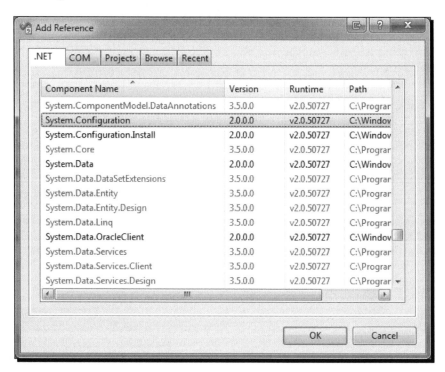

5. Next we need to add some `using` statements to the top of the class. Add the following code:

```
using System.Configuration.Provider;
using System.Security.Cryptography;
using System.Web.Security;
using Ordering.Data.DataAccess;
```

In VB.Net, we will replace `using` with `Imports` and get rid of the semicolon as follows:

```
Imports System.Configuration.Provider
Imports System.Security.Cryptography
Imports System.Web.Security
```

6. Now we need to tell our class to implement the `MembershipProvider` abstract class. After your class declaration, add the following code:

```
: System.Web.Security.MembershipProvider
```

Or in VB.NET:

```
Inherits System.Web.Security.MembershipProvider
```

7. Add the following `ValidateUser()` method to your class:

```
public override bool ValidateUser(string UserName, string
  Password)
{
  Login login = LoginDataControl.Instance.GetByUserName(UserName);
  if (login == null)
    return false;

  HMACSHA256 hash = new
    HMACSHA256(ASCIIEncoding.UTF8.GetBytes(login.Salt));
  string encodedPassword = Convert.ToBase64String
    (hash.ComputeHash(Encoding.Unicode.GetBytes(Password)));

  if (encodedPassword == login.Password && login.Active == true)
    return true;

  return false;
}
```

In VB.NET, it is as follows:

```
Public Overloads Overrides Function ValidateUser(ByVal UserName _
  As String, ByVal Password As String) As Boolean
  Dim login As Login = LoginDataControl.Instance._
    GetByUserName(UserName)
  If login Is Nothing Then
    Return False
  End If

  Dim hash As New _
    HMACSHA256(ASCIIEncoding.UTF8.GetBytes(login.Salt))
  Dim encodedPassword As String = Convert.ToBase64String _
    (hash.ComputeHash(Encoding.Unicode.GetBytes(Password)))

  If encodedPassword = login.Password AndAlso _
    login.Active = True Then
    Return True
  End If

  Return False
End Function
```

8. If you are using C#, right-click on the **MembershipProvider** definition, and select **Implement Abstract Class** to let Visual Studio "stub out" the rest of our class (VB.NET should automatically do this for us). This will create the other methods and properties required to implement the `MembershipProvider` class, with a default to throw an exception if the method is called.

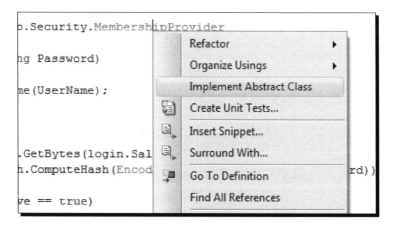

9. In the `Web.config` file, find the `<authentication>` section in the `<system. web>` block and change the authentication method from `Windows` to `Forms`.

```
<authentication mode="Forms"/>
```

10. Add a block under this to define our membership provider, giving it a type and name.

```
<membership defaultProvider="OrderingMembershipProvider">
  <providers>
    <add name="OrderingMembershipProvider"
      type="Ordering.Data.OrderingMembershipProvider,
      Ordering.Data" />
  </providers>
</membership>
```

11. That's it. Now if you start the application, you should be able to put in a username and password, and if you stop the application in Debug mode, you should be able to view the values and step through the code!

What just happened?

Now we have a working membership provider and Login controls, so let's move on to restricting what a user can see by role.

User roles

Now that we have the ability to log a user in, we can filter data based on whether or not they are logged in, and even allow access to pages based on the same. But what if we need more granular control? What if we need to only allow access to certain controls to "Administrators", or "DataManagers"? Using the `System.Web.Security.RoleProvider` abstract classes, we can extend our control to a much tighter level.

A number of controls allow restricting access to roles, but my particular favorite is the `<asp:LoginView>` control. Not only does it let us restrict a user, whether logged in or not, but it can also restrict them by role. Have a look at the following code snippet:

```
<asp:LoginView ID="loginView" runat="server">
  <AnonymousTemplate>
    <asp:Login ID="login" runat="server" />
  </AnonymousTemplate>
  <LoggedInTemplate>
    Thanks for Logging In
  </LoggedInTemplate>
</asp:LoginView>
```

Now, when you navigate to the page, if you are logged in, you will see **Thanks for Logging In** and if not, you will get an `<asp:Login>` control. This is great functionality, but not the level of control we are seeking. Lucky for us, there is another template, called `<RoleGroups>`. By defining one or more `<asp:RoleGroup>` blocks, we can restrict the data in any way we want. For example, if we want to add a new button for "Administrators" only, we can add an `<asp:RoleGroup>` block as follows:

```
<asp:LoginView ID="adminLogin" runat="server">
  <RoleGroups>
    <asp:RoleGroup Roles="Administrator">
      <ContentTemplate>
        <asp:Button ID="adminOnly" runat="server"/>
      </ContentTemplate>
    </asp:RoleGroup Roles="Administrator">
  </RoleGroups>
</asp:LoginView>
```

If we want more than one role to have access to a block, we just put the role names together, separated by a comma, into the `Roles` parameter. If we wanted to allow "Administrators" and "Data Managers" access to our button, we would just change our `<asp:RoleGroup>` statement to read as follows:

```
<asp:RoleGroup Roles="Administrator,DataManager">
```

If we needed to provide different content to different groups, we can just keep adding `<asp:RoleGroup>` blocks as necessary.

Role providers

To make our role-based controls work with NHibernate, we need to implement the `System.Web.Security.RoleProvider` abstract class. This abstract class is specifically designed to allow us to implement the ASP.NET role model using our own logic.

Just like the membership provider, the role provider has about 15 methods and properties that we can override, if we need to. However, just like the other provider, we really only need to focus on one method to implement the base class—`GetRolesForUser()`.

`GetRolesForUser()` is passed one variable, the UserName as a string, and returns an array of strings (`string[]`) containing the names of the roles to which the user belongs.

The following code snippet shows a simple NHibernate implementation of `GetRolesForUser()`:

```
public override string[] GetRolesForUser(string UserName)
{
  ArrayList roleList = new ArrayList();
  IList<Role> roles =
    RoleDataControl.Instance.GetRolesByUserName(UserName);
  foreach (Role role in roles)
  {
    roleList.Add(role.Name);
  }
  return (string[])roleList.ToArray(typeof(string));
}
```

Provider configuration

Once again, now that we have the provider written, we just need to let ASP.NET know how to use it. In the `Web.config`, under our `<membership>` block, we will add a `<roleManager>` block, once again giving it a `defaultProvider` name and telling ASP.NET to enable it:

```
<roleManager defaultProvider="OrderingRoleProvider" enabled="true">
  <providers>
    <clear/>
    <add name="OrderingRoleProvider"
      type="Ordering.Data.OrderingRoleProvider, Ordering.Data"/>
  </providers>
</roleManager>
```

Just like when we configured our membership provider, we simply have to provide a name and a type so ASP.NET can locate our custom code, and we can use all of the controls that make use of roles.

Have a go hero – using some roles

As you already have a working membership provider, why not integrate a role provider? Follow the same instructions for integrating your membership provider, but substitute the role provider instead. You will need two additional database tables, Role and Login_Role. Login_Role is a many-to-many (MTM) table between Login and Role. If you forgot how to map an MTM table, take a look at Phone and Contact. Here is the SQL for the two tables:

The Role table:

```
CREATE TABLE [dbo].[Role](
   [Id] [int] IDENTITY(1,1) NOT NULL,
   [Name] [varchar](255) NOT NULL,
   [Description] [text] NULL,
   CONSTRAINT [PK_Role] PRIMARY KEY CLUSTERED
   (
     [Id] ASC
   )
)
```

The Login_Role MTM table:

```
CREATE TABLE [dbo].[Login_Role](
   [LoginId] [int] NOT NULL,
   [RoleId] [int] NOT NULL,
   CONSTRAINT [PK_Login_Role] PRIMARY KEY CLUSTERED
   (
     [LoginId] ASC,
     [RoleId] ASC
   )
)
GO
ALTER TABLE [dbo].[Login_Role]  WITH CHECK ADD  CONSTRAINT [FK_Login_
Role_Login] FOREIGN KEY([LoginId]) REFERENCES [dbo].[Login] ([Id])
GO
ALTER TABLE [dbo].[Login_Role]  WITH CHECK ADD  CONSTRAINT [FK_Login_
Role_Role] FOREIGN KEY([RoleId]) REFERENCES [dbo].[Role] ([Id])
GO
```

Once you map your classes, add a role with the name of "Administrator" to the database, and add some logins. Don't forget to populate the Login_Role table so your users have roles, and test the whole thing out!

Summary

Now, you should have a fairly good understanding of how membership and role providers interact within ASP.NET to provide authentication and authorization as well as some of the controls you can use to interact with them.

Specifically, we talked about:

- Using the built-in membership controls:
    - The `<asp:Login>` control for user login.
    - Using the `<asp:LoginStatus>` control to display user login status.
    - Controlling viewable content with the `<asp:LoginView>` control.
- Creating and implementing a custom membership provider.
- Specifying location security using the `Web.config` file. Implementing and configuring a custom role provider.

Now that we've learned about ASP.NET Security, we're ready to talk about Code Generation, which is the topic of the next chapter.

11
It's a Generation Thing

One of the major complaints people have with using NHibernate or any ORM is all of the repetitive code they have to write. In an effort to alleviate this pain, several groups have developed code generation tools that interact with various items (the database, mapping files, or other artifacts) to generate the code required for NHibernate to operate. This can include classes, web services, data access, mapping files, and so on.

In this chapter, we'll discuss:

- ◆ Judging requirements
- ◆ CodeSmith
- ◆ nhib-gen
- ◆ AjGenesis
- ◆ Visual NHibernate
- ◆ MyGeneration
- ◆ NGen
- ◆ NHModeller
- ◆ Microsoft T4
- ◆ hbm2net

So let's get on with it.

Judging requirements

The following tools represent a sampling of the NHibernate code generation tools "in the wild" that are commonly used. This is by no means a complete list. Each product has a basic presentation of the code generation it does and a chart covering some basic requirements for an NHibernate operation. The judging criteria are as follows:

- **Editable**: Can the template, used to generate the NHibernate code, be modified?
- **Partial Classes**: Can the tool use partial classes for generating the Data Access and POCO layers?
- **N-tier**: Does the generator separate the Data Access, POCO, and Presentation layers into discrete, usable layers?
- **Data Access**: Does the generator create basic queries such as `GetByID`, `GetAll`, `GetBy(index field)`, `GetCount`, and so on?
- **MTM**: Does the generator correctly map and handle many-to-many relationships?
- **Visual Studio plugin**: Can the generator be executed from within Visual Studio?
- **Build Process add-in**: Can the generator be integrated as part of a build process?
- **Open Source**: Is the source code available for customization?

Each item will be scored on a scale of 0 to 5—0 being "No Support" and 5 meaning "Completely Supported". A sample chart is shown as follows:

Edit	Partials	N-Tier	DataAccess	MTM	VS	Build	Open Src
5	0	3	0	5	0	3	3

This table shows a tool that has a completely customizable template but does not support partial classes out of the box. It separates some of the data into separate tiers, does not generate a data access layer, correctly handles MTM tables, but doesn't have a Visual Studio plugin. The score of 3 for the Build process means that the process can be spawned from a command line, but it requires manual intervention to kick off the generation. The source code for the tool is available, but it relies on a third-party DLL that the source is not available.

All of the examples shown were generated from the Ordering database model (either imported, created manually, or from the `hbm.xml` mapping files). The model is shown in the following screenshot:

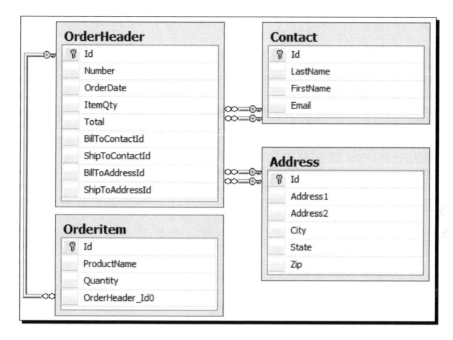

CodeSmith

One of the better known code generators on the market is CodeSmith. This tool started out as an open source tool and then went to a commercial license a few years back. You can download a trial version from `http://www.codesmithtools.com/`. Various licensing models are also available.

CodeSmith comes with a collection of NHibernate templates in the samples directory that you are free to customize to your liking. They are primarily designed to use the Visual Studio plugin to integrate into your IDE, but they work fine from either the CodeSmith Studio (a template design, compilation, and execution tool) or from the CodeSmith Explorer (a template execution tool).

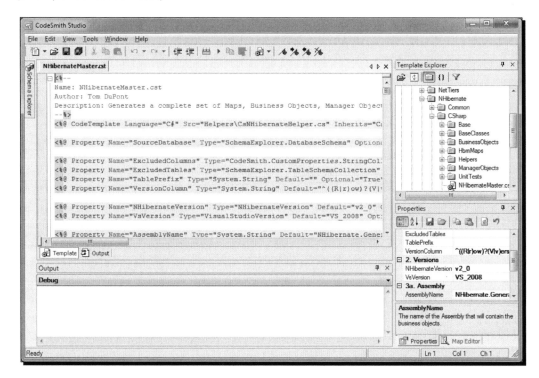

The CodeSmith templates allow you to modify many of the settings for the templates such as the `AssemblyName`, `Base Class Namespaces`, Business (POCO), Manager (DataAccess), and Unit Test namespaces.

These templates are database driven, so your model is the database and the rest of the data layer is generated from it. However, you could develop your own templates to generate from another model if you desired.

Once you get the hang of it, CodeSmith is easy to use, quick to modify, and you can tweak it to do exactly what you want.

Edit	Partials	N-Tier	DataAccess	MTM	VS	Build	Open Src
5	5	5	3	5	5	5	0

nhib-gen

The NHibernate Data Layer Generation (nhib-gen) project on SourceForge
(`http://sourceforge.net/projects/nhib-gen`) is an open source project, which
includes a set of base classes and templates to implement an entire NHibernate solution.

These templates are database-driven, so your model is the database and the rest of the data
layer is generated from it.

One caveat of nhib-gen is that you will need a CodeSmith license. Work is underway to
implement the templates in other code generation tools such as MyGeneration.

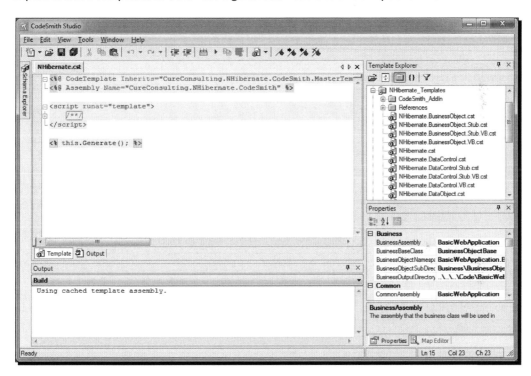

The nhib-gen project templates are the ones that I use in my development, and they have
been used by several companies for large and small projects. They combine a set of base
classes designed from "Best Practice" NHibernate documents and websites with generated
code to provide the best possible combination of performance and ease of use.

Once the basic configuration is done, nhib-gen will create a full set of common
objects (POCOs), business objects (wrappers for POCOs where you can add additional
customization), Data Access Objects, mapping files, sample ASP.NET data-bound forms,
and a full set of unit tests to exercise your data layer.

nhib-gen is extremely configurable, allowing you to generate all your files into a single DLL, separate DLLs for each layer, and so on. It will automatically add your generated files to your Visual Studio project and mark the mapping files as embedded resources.

> When I use these templates, I can have a new working data tier in as little as five minutes. I simply create a new DLL and web application project, copy the saved CodeSmith settings from another project, and search/replace the old project name with the new one to move the namespaces into the proper places. I generate the database, copy the configuration into the `Web.config`, and the application is talking to the database.

Edit	Partials	N-Tier	DataAccess	MTM	VS	Build	Open Src
5	5	5	5	5	5	5	5

AjGenesis

The AjGenesis Code Generation project is hosted on **CodePlex** (`http://ajgenesis.codeplex.com/`), and according to its author:

> *AjGenesis is an open software project that generates any text artifact, starting from free Models and Templates.*

These templates are model-driven from XML, so your model is stored in a well-formed XML file and the rest of the data layer (including the SQL for the database) is generated.

Simply put, this generator lets you define your own models and templates, so you can generate from any XML document you want.

There is an example of generating an NHibernate data layer (including the project) using your `hbm.xml` mapping files at `http://ajlopez.wordpress.com/2009/11/22/generating-code-with-ajgenesis-using-nhibernate-hbm-files/`.

The templates included in the example follow a very basic construction, much like the CodeSmith or MyGeneration style templates. Anything that needs to be rendered directly, such as the `using` statement, is simply entered in the template directly. Any variables that need to be added in, follow the `${name}` format, while code that should be executed in the template is enclosed in `<# #>` blocks.

If you look at the following template, you can see that the entire template to generate an entity from an `hbm.xml` file is only 45 lines long.

```
using System;
using System.Collections.Generic;
using Iesi.Collections.Generic;

namespace ${Entity.Namespace}
{
  public class ${Entity.ClassName} {
  <#
    for each Property in Entity.Properties where not Property.IsSet
      and not Property.IsList
  #>
  public ${Property.Type} ${Property.Name} { get; set; }
  <#
    end for

    for each Property in Entity.Properties where Property.IsSet
  #>
  public ISet<${Property.Type}> ${Property.Name} { get; set; }
  <#
    end for

    for each Property in Entity.Properties where Property.IsList
  #>
  public IList<${Property.Type}> ${Property.Name} { get; set; }
  <#
    end for
  #>

  public ${Entity.ClassName}()
  {
    <#
      for each Property in Entity.Properties where Property.IsSet
    #>
    this.${Property.Name} = new HashedSet<${Property.Type}>();
    <#
      end for

      for each Property in Entity.Properties where Property.IsList
    #>
    this.${Property.Name} = new List<${Property.Type}>();
    <#
      end for
    #>
    }
  }
}
```

Using the templates located at the previous link will generate a set of classes. I added the `partial` keyword because I prefer to be able to add code into my generated classes without modifying the generated code.

A sample `Contact` class generated from our `ordering.hbm.xml` mapping classes is as follows:

```
using System;
using System.Collections.Generic;
using Iesi.Collections.Generic;

namespace Ordering.Data
{
  public partial class Contact {
    public string Id { get; set; }
    public string FirstName { get; set; }
    public string LastName { get; set; }
    public string Email { get; set; }
    public IList<Ordering.Address> Addresses { get; set; }
    public IList<Ordering.OrderHeader> BillToOrderHeaders
      { get; set; }
    public IList<Ordering.OrderHeader> ShipToOrderHeaders
      { get; set; }
    public IList<Ordering.Phone> Phones { get; set; }

    public Contact()
    {
      this.Addresses = new List<Ordering.Address>();
      this.BillToOrderHeaders = new List<Ordering.OrderHeader>();
      this.ShipToOrderHeaders = new List<Ordering.OrderHeader>();
      this.Phones = new List<Ordering.Phone>();
    }
  }
}
```

Overall, this is a very simple-to-use, flexible code generation engine.

Edit	Partials	N-Tier	DataAccess	MTM	VS	Build	Open Src
5	4	1[1]	0[1]	5	2[2]	5	5

1. The sample templates only generate POCOs, but other templates could be quickly added.

2. The console application can be integrated with Visual Studio as a pre-build step.

Visual NHibernate

Another way to look at your NHibernate project is to use a visual modeler, such as Visual NHibernate from **Slyce Software** (http://www.slyce.com/VisualNHibernate/).

This generator is model-driven, so your model is created and stored inside your project, and the data layer and scripts for the database are generated. Models can be created from existing databases, existing NHibernate projects (source code), or from scratch.

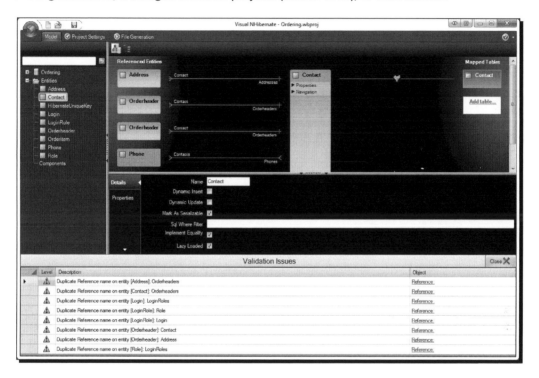

Edit	Partials	N-Tier	DataAccess	MTM	VS	Build	Open Src
5	3	4	5	5	5	0	0

MyGeneration

One of the best code generators out there is MyGeneration. It is open source and free (as in zero cost). You can get the latest version from http://www.mygenerationsoftware.com or from the **SourceForge** project page at http://sourceforge.net/projects/mygeneration.

According to their SourceForge page:

> *MyGeneration is an extremely flexible template-based code generator written in Microsoft.NET. MyGeneration is great at generating code for ORM architectures. The metadata from your database is made available to the templates through the MyMeta API.*

The MyGeneration templates are typically database-driven, so your model is stored in the database and the rest of the data layer is generated.

MyGeneration has a very clean, simple interface, and is very user-friendly. As an added bonus, if you don't like the way a feature works, remember, it's open source, so you can download the source code and change it!

Much like CodeSmith, MyGeneration uses templates to render the code it generates. Therefore, you can create your own templates or modify one that someone else has shared. MyGeneration has a large set of templates for you to use and more are available at `http://www.mygenerationsoftware.com/templatelibrary/default.aspx`.

One of my favorite NHibernate templates was uploaded by Daniel Lujan (lujan99 on the MyGeneration site). This template is called "NHibernate lujan99 – 1.0.6" and can be downloaded from `http://www.mygenerationsoftware.com/TemplateLibrary/Download/?templateid=20584a7d-cad9-4e84-86eb-2da504d64781`.

I would only make two small changes to this excellent template. The first is to add the keyword `partial` on line 4751.

The original code at line 4751 is as follows:

```
str.AppendLine(" public class <xsl:value-of select=\"$classname\"/>
    <xsl:if test=\"string-length($inheritFrom)>0\"> :
    <xsl:value-of select=\"$inheritFrom\"/> </xsl:if>");
```

After making the changes, the new code at line 4751 is as follows:

```
str.AppendLine(" public partial class
  <xsl:value-of select=\"$classname\"/>
  <xsl:if test=\"string-length($inheritFrom)>0\"> :
  <xsl:value-of select=\"$inheritFrom\"/> </xsl:if>");
```

The other change would be to modify the generated class filename to end with
.generated.cs instead of .cs. This needs to happen on lines 3674 and 3696.

The original code at line 3696 is as follows:

```
nx.Attributes["name"].Value.Replace(" ", "") )+ ".cs"),
```

The updated code at line 3696 is as follows:

```
nx.Attributes["name"].Value.Replace(" ", "") )+ ".generated.cs"),
```

The original code at line 3674 is as follows:

```
Path.Combine(_path2Src,name+".cs"),
```

The updated code at line 3674 is as follows:

```
Path.Combine(_path2Src,name+".generated.cs"),
```

These changes will allow us to create another partial class to contain our own custom
properties that wouldn't get overwritten the next time we generate by creating a new partial
class with the same name, such as Address.cs, to go along with Address.generated.cs.

Edit	Partials	N-Tier	DataAccess	MTM	VS	Build	Open Src
5	3	5	0	5	0	5	5

Time for action – using MyGeneration

Let's see how much time using MyGeneration and the L99-NHibernate template would have
saved us by generating our POCOs and mapping files.

1. If you haven't already done so, download MyGeneration from
   http://sourceforge.net/projects/mygeneration/ and install it.

2. Download the L99-NHibernate template from http://www.
   mygenerationsoftware.com/TemplateLibrary/Download/
   ?templateid=20584a7d-cad9-4e84-86eb-2da504d64781 and place it into
   the Templates folder of the MyGeneration installation (usually c:\Program
   Files\MyGeneration13\Templates).

3. Start MyGeneration from either the **Start** menu or by directly running `MyGeneration.exe`.

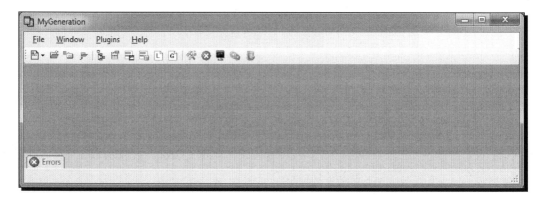

4. The first time you run it, MyGeneration will present the **Default Settings** window. In this window, under **Connection String**, add the following connection string:

```
Provider=SQLOLEDB.1;Integrated Security=SSPI;Initial
Catalog=ordering;Data Source=.\sqlexpress
```

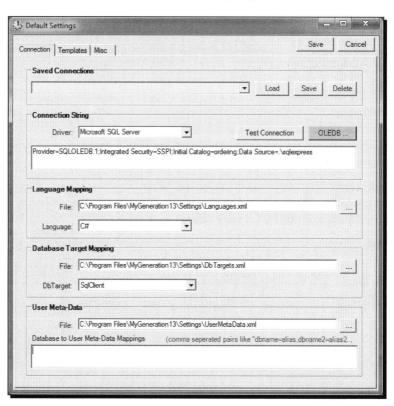

5. In the **Saved Connections** box, type the name **local**, and click on the **Save** button.

6. Load the L99-NHibernate template (`199_nhibernate.csgen`) using the **File | Open** menu.

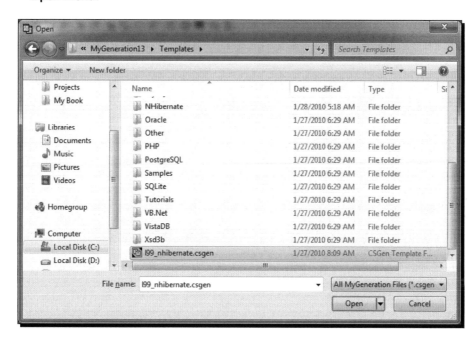

7. Once the template has loaded, start the template by pressing *F5*, selecting **Template | Execute**, or hitting the green arrow in the toolbar. The template will compile and show a window with three tabs: **Tables**, **Options**, and **Help**.

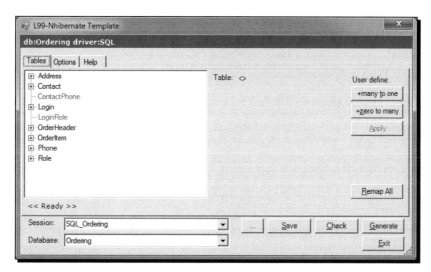

8. Click on the **Options** tab, change the **Class Assembly** and **Class Namespace** to **Ordering.Data**, and change the **Output path** to your code directory.

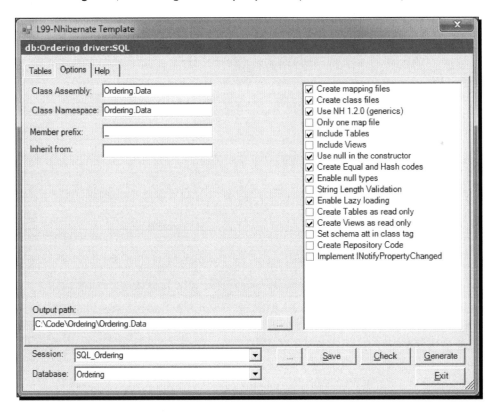

9. Click on the **Generate** button and MyGeneration will generate your classes. When it is complete, you should get a confirmation box similar to the one shown in the following screenshot:

10. Your target directory will now have two new folders, `Entities` and `Mappings`, which contain the POCOs and `hbm.xml` mapping files, as shown in the following screenshot:

What just happened?

With a few simple clicks, we have created the basis for our NHibernate database interaction. All we need to do now is put together some data access classes and we are ready to use them!

NGen NHibernate Code Generator

Another open source NHibernate code generator that you can use is the NGen NHibernate Code Generator, hosted on SourceForge at `http://sourceforge.net/projects/ngennhibernatec/`.

This project does a basic generation of POCOs (DAO classes) and mapping files, as well as creating data access classes (Services). This tool is also open source, written in C#, so you can download it and make any changes to it that you like.

It doesn't appear to have any command-line options for generation or have a Visual Studio plugin, but you could integrate them pretty easily.

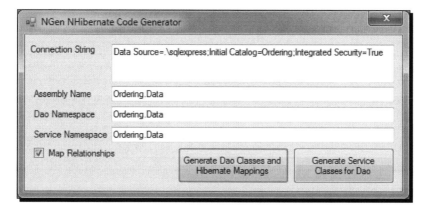

Edit	Partials	N-Tier	DataAccess	MTM	VS	Build	Open Src
4	1	4	5	0	0	0	5

NHModeller

Another interesting project is the NHModeller tool. While I generally use the database to represent my model, this tool decouples the model from the data structure in a very slick manner. All we need to do is define our model in a text file and use either the command-line application or a plugin for the free Intellipad tool from Microsoft to generate POCO's, HBM. XML files, and SQL Scripts.

More information on this product is available at `http://nhmodeller.selfip.com/`.

This tool generates data from a model. However, instead of using a visual representation (such as Visual NHibernate), it uses a text-based **Domain Specific Language (DSL)** to describe the entities.

A simple `Contact` object model would look something as follows:

```
NHModel
{
  Entity Contact
  {
    LastName:string(255)
    FirstName:string(255)
    Email:string(255)
  } in Contact
}
```

One nice feature of this product is the Intellipad plugin. This plugin provides basic IntelliSense and syntax highlighting, as well as the option to run the generation from within the editing environment.

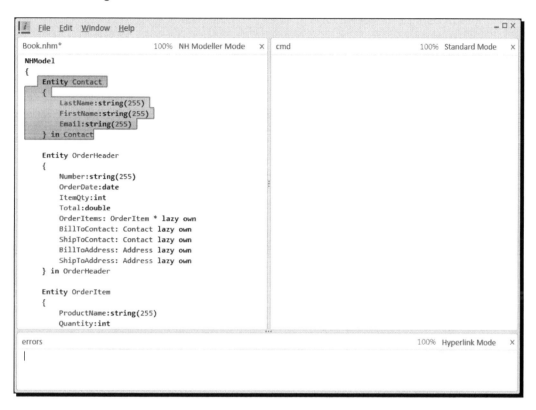

Once we have created the model, we can generate the code from the NHModeller plugin, which prompts us for some parameters, such as the **Assembly name**, the **Prefix for generated code files**, database connection information, and so on, as shown in the following screenshot:

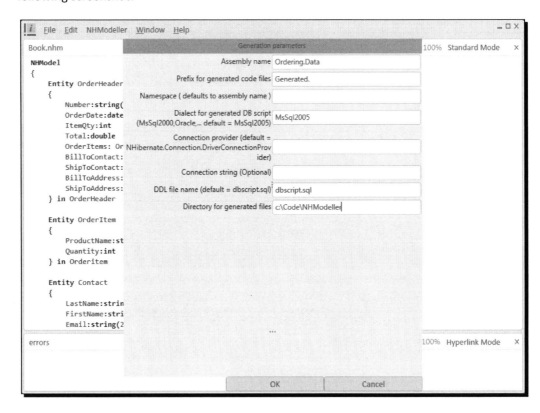

Once we have entered all of the generation parameters, the product will generate all of the POCOs, mapping classes, and SQL scripts.

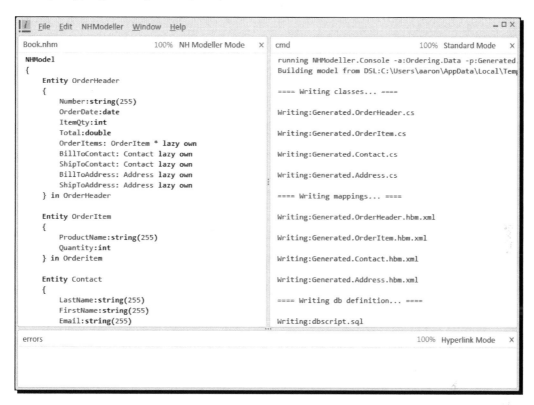

Overall, I think this is an interesting tool, and while still in its infancy, it has a lot of potential for developers who want to decouple their model from their data storage mechanism.

Edit	Partials	N-Tier	DataAccess	MTM	VS	Build	Open Src
0	5	1[1]	0[1]	5	2[2]	5	0

1. NHModeller only generates POCOs, SQL scripts, and Mapping files.

2. The console application can be integrated with Visual Studio as a pre-build step.

Microsoft T4 templates

Another emerging code generation engine is the one Microsoft included in the Visual Studio IDE to autogenerate the behind-the-scene classes for their LINQ and Entity Framework frameworks. These templates integrate with the IDE or can be hosted outside the IDE with custom code. There doesn't seem to be a lot of NHibernate-specific templates at the moment, but they are starting to emerge and should be better supported in the future.

Edit	Partials	N-Tier	DataAccess	MTM	VS	Build	Open Src
4	0	1	3	0	5	5	0

T4 hbm2net

Officially part of the NHibernate project (in the NHibernate-Contrib section), the T4 hbm2net project will generate .NET classes from `hbm.xml` mapping files. Running the console application `hbm2net.exe` and passing in the name of the `hbm.xml` mapping files (`*.hbm.xml`), the application will generate partial classes with all of the mapped fields. As this is a templated generator, you can "tweak" the template to output the generated classes in any way that you would like them.

This generator creates classes using the `hbm.xml` mapping files as a model for the POCOs. It can be coupled with the hbm2ddl project to generate database scripts, or you can use the ddl2hbm tool to generate the `hbm.xml` files.

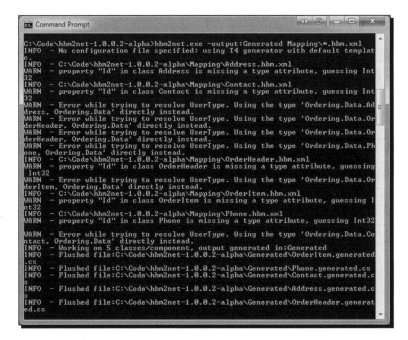

In the previous screenshot, you can see the results of generating classes from the mapping files from the `Ordering.Data` (in the Mapping folder) being generated into a folder named `Generated`.

You can find out more about this generator at `http://nhforge.org/blogs/nhibernate/archive/2009/12/12/t4-hbm2net-alpha-2.aspx`.

Edit	Partials	N-Tier	DataAccess	MTM	VS	Build	Open Src
5	5	1[1]	3	5	2[2]	5	5

1. The application only generates POCOs.
2. The console application can be integrated with Visual Studio as a pre-build step.

Summary

In this chapter, we discussed some of the benefits of NHibernate code generators and the ways to reduce the overhead of creating classes and manually mapping our database to our POCOs.

Specifically, we covered the judging requirements for each of the generation engines, and how they were compared. We also discussed each of the following NHibernate code generation/modeling engines: CodeSmith, NHib-GenAj, Genesis, Visual NHibernate, MyGeneration, NGen, NHModeller, Microsoft T4, and hbm2net.

We also talked about the pros and cons of each of these generation engines, and hopefully you have enough information to start looking at some of these to figure out which one is the best for you.

Now that we know about some of the template engines, we're ready to talk about some general .NET Tools, Best Practices, and methodologies, which is the topic of the next chapter.

12
Odds and Ends

This section could have been called "Little Bits", "Random Thoughts", or anything else to convey the idea that, even though they may not be very cohesive, they are the pieces I use all the time, which may not have had a perfect place anywhere else.

In this chapter, we'll talk about:

- Unit of Work and Burrow
- maxRequestLength
- Blog.Net
- Converting CSS Templates
- XML Documentation and GhostDoc

Let's dive right in.

Unit of Work and Burrow

In Martin Fowler's Patterns of Enterprise Application Architecture, he describes the concept of Unit of Work. A basic description of the Unit of Work pattern can be found at `http://www.martinfowler.com/eaaCatalog/unitOfWork.html`.

> *When you're pulling data in and out of a database, it's important to keep track of what you've changed. Otherwise, that data won't be written back into the database. Similarly, you have to insert the new objects you create and remove any objects you delete.*

One way to think of this is to think back to our order. In our traditional model, creating an order would involve something like this:

1. Create Bill/Ship Contact.
2. Create Order Header | associate Contact(s).
3. Create Order Items | associate to Order Header.
4. Total Order Items, Update Order Header.

Each of these actions would most likely be performed in a discrete database transaction.

In a Unit of Work pattern, "Insert a new Order" would be a single unit of work. Each of the items required to create or modify the order would be gathered and the Save or Update actions would take place only when that particular Unit of Work needs to be persisted.

In order to implement this pattern using the NHibernate session, we need to decouple ourselves from the ASP.NET stateless postback model because, to create an order, we might need to retrieve data from several pages in order to construct our order.

One of the frameworks you can use to help implement this pattern is the Burrow framework, which helps to provide stateful NHibernate session management in ASP.NET.

You can find out more information about this framework and how to use it at `http://nhforge.org/wikis/burrow/home.aspx`.

The major change between our previous implementations and the Burrow framework is that we need to allow Burrow to manage our sessions, as shown by the following code.

```
ISession session = new BurrowFramework().GetSession();
```

Burrow implements the Conversation concept. For conversations that can be handled in a single transaction (a single web page post), Burrow will handle the transaction automatically. For more involved conversations, Burrow provides the long conversation. You can read more about the long conversation at `http://nhforge.org/wikis/burrow/conversation-explained.aspx`.

Pop quiz – doing the thing

1. What is the core concept of the Unit of Work pattern?

   a. Small, discrete updates

   b. Business Transactions

   c. Database Layout Optimization

   d. None of the above.

2. What does the Burrow framework provide?

    a. Unit of Work Business Logic

    b. Advance e-mail capabilities

    c. NHibernate session management

How does this relate to NHibernate?

As you read through the rest of this chapter, you might be asking yourself that exact question, and I don't blame you. Several of these topics have NOTHING (or at least very little) to do with NHibernate directly.

They are included because they are things that I use, day in and day out, to make my NHibernate projects easier, faster, more maintainable, or simply better.

Blog.Net blogging components

Most developers have a website and most of us have a blog. The primary issue with most blogging software is that it is a standalone product, either requiring you to completely revamp your website to integrate it, let IT manage your website, or worse, run on a totally separate server and not be integrated with your current website at all.

The Blog.Net project aims to correct that issue by providing simple-to-use, server-side ASP.NET components that you can "drop" onto a page and forget about. There are controls for "Top X" entries, "Latest X" entries, and so on.

This project uses NHibernate as the data-retrieval mechanism and will work against any data source that NHibernate can access, allowing YOU to specify how your blog works for YOU, and not vice-versa.

The Blog.Net project can be accessed on CodePlex at `http://blogdotnet.codeplex.com/`

maxRequestLength

One of the ways an attacker can get into your site is by attempting to cause a "buffer overflow" or by creating a denial of service by sending large amounts of data to your server. This can also be a problem if you have an `<asp:FileUpload>` control on one of your pages because the attacker could upload large files one after another until the disk space is filled, possibly causing your server to error out.

One way to help protect yourself from these types of attacks is to set a `maxRequestLength`. The `maxRequestLength` is a filter, rejecting user requests that are larger than the threshold set. For instance, the default setting in your `Machine.config` file is set to 4096 KB or 4 MB. Ninety-nine percent of all your pages will be well below that, probably more likely in the 512 KB or less range.

To protect yourself, add an `<httpRuntime>` directive in the `<system.web>` section of the `Web.config`, and set the `maxRequestLength` to a reasonable value.

```
<system.web>
  <httpRuntime maxRequestLength="512" />

</system.web>
```

If you do need a larger value for something such as a `<asp:FileUpload>` control on a page, then change the value for that particular page only. You can do this easily by using a `<location>` tag.

The following code snippet shows the use of the `<location>` tag to allow uploads of up to 2 MB to the `UploadFile.aspx` page:

```
<location path="~/UploadFile.aspx">
  <system.web>
    <httpRuntime maxRequestLength="2048" />
  </system.web>
</location>
```

By using this simple tag, you can really restrict the types of attacks that can be executed against your web application.

Converting CSS templates

One thing I do ALL THE TIME is use master pages and themes to provide constant theming to my websites. One thing I am NOT, however, is a graphic designer. I have great respect for someone that can take a blank canvas and turn it into something great to look at, but I know I am not that person.

Several of the folks that are quite good at creating these types of products have opened them up to the world to use freely on the websites they create. Many of these templates use **Cascading Style Sheets (CSS)** to effectively lay out the images and data they want to display. A quick search for "Free CSS Templates" will return a number of places to download these templates that are generally free to use. You can use them anywhere you want. In exchange, you'll have to leave an attribution on the page, usually in the footer.

One of my favorite sites to find these templates is `http://www.freecsstemplates.org`. This site has literally hundreds of templates that can be converted into master page and theme with a few simple keystrokes. The basic concept is as follows:

◆ Create a master page

◆ Create an ASP.NET theme

◆ Migrate the CSS information from the template into the theme

◆ Copy the HTML from the template into the master page

◆ Replace the default content of the template with `<asp:ContentPlaceHolder>` regions

As you will see in the following *Time for action*, this is a really simple process to make the creating our websites both quicker and more visually pleasing.

Time for action – converting a CSS template

For this example, I am going to use the "Clean Type" CSS template from *freeCSStemplates. org* (on the Internet).

1. Download the "Clean Type" template from `http://www.freecsstemplates.org/download/zip/cleantype`. Save this ZIP file somewhere on your local machine. The "Clean Type" template looks as shown in the following screenshot:

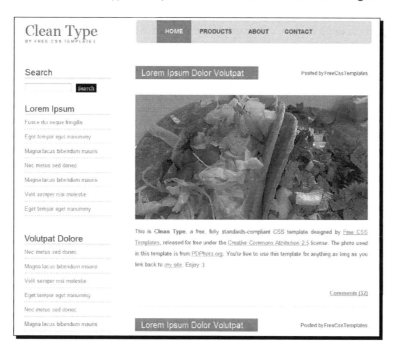

2. Extract the files from the `cleantype.zip` archive using WinZip, WinRAR, or your favorite ZIP extraction tool by right-clicking on the file and then clicking on **Extract All**.

3. Once you unzip it, inside two nested directories, you will find all the files. There are three files and a directory of five images. If you double-click on the `index.html` file, it should open in your browser and look as shown in the previous screenshot.

4. Open Visual Studio and create a new Web Application project from **File | New | Project**, and select **ASP.NET Web Application**. Use any project name and solution name you like such as **CSSTestApp.Web** and **CSSTestApp**.

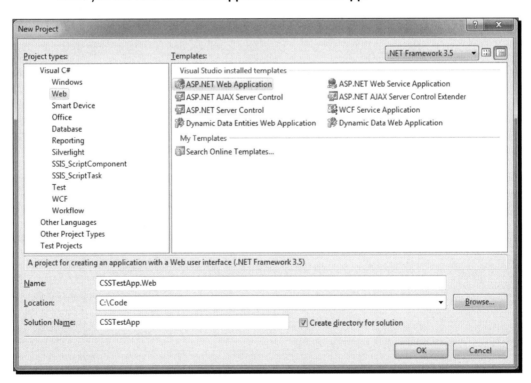

5. Next, we will delete the `Default.aspx` page and the `App_Data` folders, as we won't need either of these.

6. Right-click on the **CSSTestApp.Web** project, and click **Add | New Folder**. Name the folder **App_MasterPages**.

7. Right-click on the **App_MasterPages** folder, and select **Add | New Item**.

8. From the **Add New Item** dialog box, select **Master Page**, and name it **CleanType. Master**, as shown in the following screenshot:

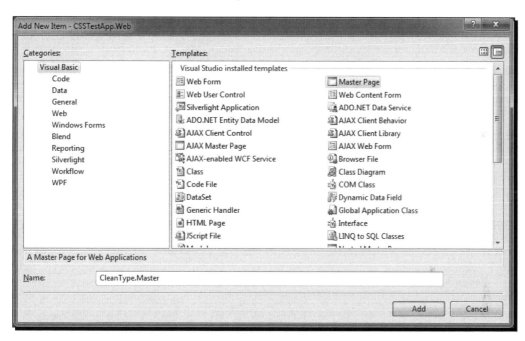

9. Inside the `CleanType.Master` page, remove the `<asp:ContentPlaceholder>` with the ID of "head" from the `<head>` section.

10. Inside the body section, remove everything inside the `<form>` tags. When you are done, your file should look as follows:

```
<%@ Master Language="C#" AutoEventWireup="true"
  CodeBehind="CleanType.master.cs"
  Inherits="CSSTestApp.Web.App_MasterPages.CleanType" %>

<!DOCTYPE html PUBLIC "-//W3C//DTD XHTML 1.0 Transitional//EN"
  "http://www.w3.org/TR/xhtml1/DTD/xhtml1-transitional.dtd">
<html xmlns="http://www.w3.org/1999/xhtml">
  <head runat="server">
    <title></title>
```

```
      </head>
      <body>
        <form id="form1" runat="server">
        </form>
      </body>
</html>
```

11. Now, we need to convert our `index.html` file into a master page. Drag the `index.html` file from the folder into Visual Studio, and drop it into the large editing space in the middle. This will open the file without adding it to our project.

12. Next, we copy everything between the `<body>` and `</body>` tags from the `index.html` file and paste it inside our `<form>` and `</form>` tags in the `CleanType.Master` file. You can close the `index.html` file now, as we are done with it.

13. Now all we need to do is stick in a few `<asp:ContentPlaceHolder>` sections so we can specify our own content in our pages. Search in the file for a `<div>` with the `id` of "content". It should be followed by a `<div class="post">`. Insert a new line under the `<div id="content">` line and add:

`<asp:ContentPlaceHolder ID="main" runat="server" />`

14. Now find a `<div>` with the `id` of "sidebar". It should be followed by a `<ul>`. Insert a new line under the `<div id="sidebar">` line, and add:

`<asp:ContentPlaceHolder ID="sideBar" runat="server" />`

15. Save our new master page, then right-click on the **CSSTestApp.Web** project, and add another new item—this time a **Web Content Form**. Name this form `Default.aspx` and click on **Add**.

16. Visual Studio will prompt us to **Select a Master Page**. Select the **App_MasterPages** folder, and select the **CleanType.Master** page.

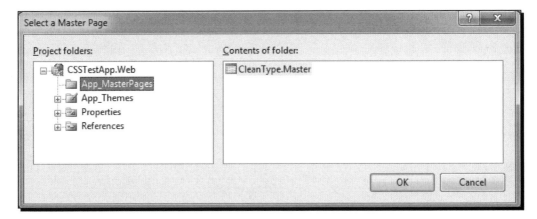

17. Open our new `Default.aspx` page, and you should have two pre-defined `<asp:Content>` tags. Let's copy the sample information out of the `CleanType.Master` page into these regions.

In the `CleanType.Master`, find the `<asp:ContentPlaceHolder>` with the ID of "main" that we just created. Under this line, there is a `<div class="post">`. Select the "-" on the left of the line to collapse this section. Underneath it, there is another `<div class="post">` section. Collapse it as well.

18. Select both of these sections, and press *Ctrl* + *X* to remove them.

19. Now, go back to our `Default.aspx` page, and inside the `<asp:Content>` tag with the `ContentPlaceHolderID` of "main", paste the two sections we just cut out of the `CleanType.Master` with *Ctrl* + *V*.

20. Cut the entire `<ul>` section from the `CleanType.Master` under the `<asp:ContentPlaceHolder>` tag with the Id of "sideBar", and paste it into the `Default.aspx` in the `<asp:Content>` section with the `ContentPlaceHolderID` of "sideBar".

21. Right-click on the **CSSTEstApp.Web** project again, and click **Add | Add ASP.NET Folder | Theme**, as shown in the following screenshot. Visual Studio will add a new folder called **App_Themes** with a child folder named **Theme1**.

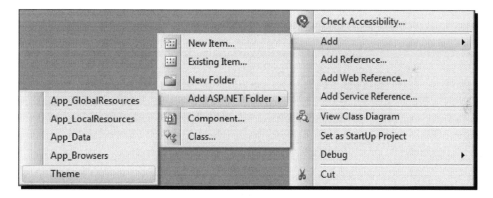

22. Change the theme folder name from `Theme1` to `CleanType`.

23. In the **cleantype** directory that contains our CSS template files, copy the `default.css` and `images` folder, and paste them into our `CleanType` theme in our `CSSTestApp.Web` application.

You can just press *Ctrl + C* on the file and the folder, then select the `CleanType` theme folder in Visual Studio and press *Ctrl + V* or right-click and select **Paste**.

24. Rename the `images` folder to `Images` (just capitalize the "I").

25. Rename the `default.css` file to `CleanType.css`.

26. Open the `CleanType.css` file and search for **url(images/** and replace it with **url(Images/**.

 While this step is not critical for applications hosted in IIS, we definitely need to do it for Mono or other systems where the filesystem is case sensitive.

27. Open the `Web.config` file, and search for the `<pages>` tag. This is where we need to tell ASP.NET to use our theme files.

```
<pages theme="CleanType">
```

28. In this particular template, the images `img02.jpg` and `img03.jpg` are actually content images.

 We can handle these images by either creating a `Skin` file inside the `CleanType` theme folder and creating `SkinID` aliases for these images in our folder, or by just moving them to a new root folder called `Images`.

As the second method is simpler, let's do that. Right-click on the **CSSTestApp.Web** project again, and click **Add | New Folder** and name it **Images**.

29. Open the `Images` folder inside the `CleanType` theme folder, and select `img02.jpg` and `img03.jpg`. Drag them to the new **Images** folder we created to move them there.

30. Press *F5* or select **Debug | Start Debugging** and our new CSS Templated Web Application using Master Pages and Themes should appear, looking just like the original.

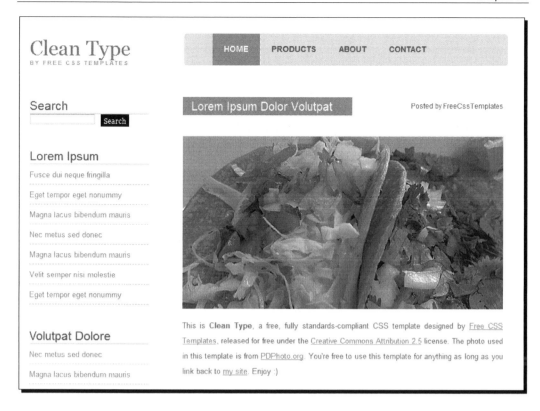

What just happened?

Within a few minutes time, we were able to convert a simple ASP.NET web application into something aesthetically pleasing. From here, all we need to do is create our content. To create new pages, we just create a new page using **Add New Item | Web Content Form** and add new content using the CSS classes such as "post", "title", "byline", "entry", and so on.

Have a go hero – .NETing the master page

Another thing we could do is convert the menu `<ul>` section in the `<div id="menu">` to an `<asp:Menu Orientation="Horizontal">` menu control and convert the `<image>` tags to `<asp:Image>` tags. We should also modify the CSS file to support our new `<asp:Menu>` control instead of the old `<ul>` and `<li>` tags.

In the CSS file, there is an element "#menu ul". This is the menu wrapper. Replace the "#menu ul" with "#menu .header" to turn this into a CSS class name that we can use in our menu control.

A simple replacement for this menu control would look as follows:

```
<div id="menu">
  <asp:Menu Orientation="Horizontal" SkipLinkText="" runat="server">
    <StaticMenuStyle CssClass="header" />
    <StaticSelectedStyle CssClass="active" />
    <Items>
      <asp:MenuItem Text="Home" NavigateUrl="~/Default.aspx"
        Selected="true" />
      <asp:MenuItem Text="Products" NavigateUrl="~/Products.aspx" />
      <asp:MenuItem Text="About" NavigateUrl="~/About.aspx" />
      <asp:MenuItem Text="Contact" NavigateUrl="~/Contact.aspx" />
    </Items>
  </asp:Menu>
</div>
```

XML documentation & GhostDoc

GhostDoc is a great little tool, originally written by Roland Weigelt, which helps you to maintain the XML documents in your code. You can download it from its new home at SubMain, the Developer Tools Division of vbCity.com, LLC.

I'm sure you've seen those great-looking comments preceded by the /// in C# or the ''' in VB.NET, that once written, will provide not only us but anyone else that uses our code IntelliSense information.

Take, for instance, our method to get the roles for a user:

```
public override string[] GetRolesForUser(string UserName)
```

Taken out of context, this doesn't really tell us much about what the method does. However, if we add some XML documentation to it, it can be much more informative:

```
/// <summary>
/// Retrieves a string[] of Roles for a user with given UserName
/// </summary>
/// <param name="UserName">The login name of the user</param>
/// <returns>string[] of role names</returns>
public override string[] GetRolesForUser(string UserName)
```

Now we know a lot more about the method just by reading the comments, but in the words of the illustrious Ginsu knife commercials, "But wait! There's more!". If we actually use this method, we will now get IntelliSense information about our method, as shown in the following screenshot:

```
provider.GetRolesForUser(|
string[] OrderingRoleProvider.GetRolesForUser (string UserName)
UserName:
    The login name of the user
```

Probably, the main reason most people don't use these comments is the sheer volume of work it takes to write them. When you hit /// in C#, it will insert a default comment, but unfortunately it doesn't provide any useful information.

```
/// <summary>
///
/// </summary>
/// <param name="UserName"></param>
/// <returns></returns>
public override string[] GetRolesForUser(string UserName)
```

However, by using GhostDoc instead of using ///, we press the default key combination of *CTRL + Shift + D* (for document) and it inserts the comment as follows:.

```
/// <summary>
/// Gets the roles for user.
/// </summary>
/// <param name="UserName">Name of the user.</param>
/// <returns></returns>
public override string[] GetRolesForUser(string UserName)
```

It works just as neatly in VB.NET:

```
''' <summary>
''' Gets the roles for user.
''' </summary>
''' <param name="UserName">Name of the user.</param>
''' <returns></returns>
Public Overloads Overrides Function GetRolesForUser _
    (ByVal UserName As String) As String()
```

This comment is nearly identical to the one that I created by hand earlier, and all it took was a quick three-finger key chord. We can run through the document pressing *CTRL + Shift + D* on each of our methods and have usable documentation in minutes.

Summary

We learned a lot in this chapter about a few random topics to help you implement NHibernate, ASP.NET web applications, and .NET applications in general.

Specifically, we talked about:

- Implementing the Unit of Work patterns by using the Burrow framework
- Using the `maxRequestLength` parameter to help protect us from buffer overflow and other security issues
- Accessing controls from the Blog.Net project to integrate our blog directly into our ASP.NET website
- Converting CSS templates into ASP.NET master pages and themes to directly integrate them with our website and give them a more ASP.NET "feel"
- Writing XML documentation to make our code more readable, usable, and maintainable, and using GhostDoc to automate much of that process, so that it isn't such a burden

Pop Quiz Answers

Chapter 2 – Database Layout and Design

Relationships

Question number	Answer
1	D – OTS is not a relational database relationship type.
2	A – A many-to-many (MTM) database relationship is modeled in an additional table.
3	D – Left, right, and inner joins are all valid.

Chapter 3 – A Touch of Class

Mapping

Question number	Answer
1	B – We use Nullable types (`int?` or `Nullable(of Integer)`) to map nullable fields when a native type like `int` or `DateTime` doesn't allow nulls.
2	Parent-child relationship properties are mapped using lists of objects (`IList<>` or `IList(of t)`) where the actual name of the object is placed between the `<>` in C# or in place of the `t` in VB.
3	A or B – This is a kind of a trick question, as you don't technically have to have a default constructor (.NET will generate one behind the scenes), but you really should have at least one constructor

Chapter 4 – Data Cartography

Class mapping

Question number	Answer
1	B – Name is the only required attribute, but name and type are the most commonly used.
2	D – The class property needs the name of the class and the table name to correctly map it.

Chapter 5 – The Session Procession

Creating and updating records

Question number	Answer
1	C – The Session Factory is used to create new sessions.
2	D – All of the listed methods will commit a record to the database, with different permutations. A will insert the record as a new record. B will attempt to update the record, assuming that it exists. C will save it if it is new, or update it if it exists.
3	C – The Delete() command removes a record from the database.

Chapter 6 – I'm Logger

Logging

Question number	Answer
1	A – We use appenders to dequeue messages from log4net and make them visible to us.
2	D – All of these are technically correct. Priority and Level are interchangeable level filters and the Filter tag on an appender can perform this function also.
3	D – That's right, we have SEVERAL ways to configure log4net. We can configure it using XML in the App.config or Web.config file, in a separate XML file, or in code inside our application.

Chapter 7 – Configuration

Basic configuration

Question number	Answer
1	A– By using the connection string name from the `<connectionStrings>` section we can encrypt that section and protect our connection strings settings.
2	C – The driver class is automatically set by the `dialect` property and doesn't usually need to be set.
3	A – The `proxyfactory.factory_class` is used to lazily load records.

Chapter 8 – Writing Queries

Fieldnames and ICriteria

Question number	Answer
1	B – We use the FieldNames structure to provide a consistent property name to our criteria queries.
2	C – We use the `criteria.List<T>()` to return a strongly typed List of type `<T>` containing the objects that matched our filtering criteria.
3	C – The `UniqueResult<T>()` method will return exactly one record, or null. No more, no less.

Chapter 9 – Binding Data

Basic data binding

Question number	Answer
1	A – Templated controls provide the most flexibility because they can be composed of any other controls, HTML, script, and so on.
2	A, B, and C – We can either use the `DataSource` property and bind records directory to the control or use the `DataSourceID` property to specify the name of the control that will provide the data.
3	A – The `Eval()` (or `DataBinder.Eval()`) method can be used to bind data to a templated control.

Chapter 10 – .NET Security

Access configuration

Question number	Answer
1	B – The asterisk (*) is used to denote all users.
2	D – We can use any or all of these to control authorization within our Web.config file.
3	B – Only authenticated users will be allowed into the website because we are denying all anonymous users.

Chapter 12 – Odds and Ends

Burrowing in

Question number	Answer
1	B – The main point of the Unit of Work pattern is to apply updates to the core business idea, not the individual objects. By using this pattern, we reduce the number of small database transactions, which can slow down an application.
2	C – Burrow provides advances NHibernate session management in the form of a conversation, which helps us to make business idea changes and not just individual record changes.

Index

Thank you for buying
NHibernate 2 Beginner's Guide

About Packt Publishing

Packt, pronounced 'packed', published its first book "*Mastering phpMyAdmin for Effective MySQL Management*" in April 2004 and subsequently continued to specialize in publishing highly focused books on specific technologies and solutions.

Our books and publications share the experiences of your fellow IT professionals in adapting and customizing today's systems, applications, and frameworks. Our solution based books give you the knowledge and power to customize the software and technologies you're using to get the job done. Packt books are more specific and less general than the IT books you have seen in the past. Our unique business model allows us to bring you more focused information, giving you more of what you need to know, and less of what you don't.

Packt is a modern, yet unique publishing company, which focuses on producing quality, cutting-edge books for communities of developers, administrators, and newbies alike. For more information, please visit our website: www.packtpub.com.

About Packt Open Source

In 2010, Packt launched two new brands, Packt Open Source and Packt Enterprise, in order to continue its focus on specialization. This book is part of the Packt Open Source brand, home to books published on software built around Open Source licences, and offering information to anybody from advanced developers to budding web designers. The Open Source brand also runs Packt's Open Source Royalty Scheme, by which Packt gives a royalty to each Open Source project about whose software a book is sold.

Writing for Packt

We welcome all inquiries from people who are interested in authoring. Book proposals should be sent to author@packtpub.com. If your book idea is still at an early stage and you would like to discuss it first before writing a formal book proposal, contact us; one of our commissioning editors will get in touch with you.

We're not just looking for published authors; if you have strong technical skills but no writing experience, our experienced editors can help you develop a writing career, or simply get some additional reward for your expertise.

Spring Persistence with Hibernate

ISBN: 978-1-849510-56-1   Paperback: 460 pages

Build robust and reliable persistence solutions for your enterprise Java application

1. Get to grips with Hibernate and its configuration manager, mappings, types, session APIs, queries, and much more

2. Integrate Hibernate and Spring as part of your enterprise Java stack development

3. Work with Spring IoC (Inversion of Control), Spring AOP, transaction management, web development, and unit testing considerations and features

4. Covers advanced and useful features of Hibernate in a practical way

ASP.NET 3.5 Application Architecture and Design

ISBN: 978-1-847195-50-0   Paperback: 300 pages

Build solid, scalable ASP.NET applications quickly and easily

1. Master the architectural options in ASP.NET to enhance your applications

2. Develop and implement n-tier architecture to allow you to modify a component without disturbing the next one

3. Design scalable and maintainable web applications rapidly

4. Implement ASP.NET MVC framework to manage various components independently

Please check **www.PacktPub.com** for information on our titles

Entity Framework Tutorial

ISBN: 978-1-847195-22-7 Paperback: 228 pages

Learn to build a better data access layer with the ADO.NET Entity Framework and ADO.NET Data Services

1. Clear and concise guide to the ADO.NET Entity Framework with plentiful code examples

2. Create Entity Data Models from your database and use them in your applications

3. Learn about the Entity Client data provider and create statements in Entity SQL

4. Learn about ADO.NET Data Services and how they work with the Entity Framework

Apache CXF Web Service Development

ISBN: 978-1-847195-40-1 Paperback: 268 pages

Develop and deploy SOAP and RESTful Web Services

1. Design and develop web services using contract-first and code-first approaches

2. Publish web services using various CXF frontends such as JAX-WS and Simple frontend

3. Invoke services by configuring CXF transportss

4. Create custom interceptors by implementing advanced features such as CXF Interceptors, CXF Invokers, and CXF Features

5. The first practical guide on Apache CXF with real-world examples

Please check **www.PacktPub.com** for information on our titles